REDESIGNING PROSPERITY

A Blueprint for Sustainable Progress

DR. MEENAKSHI SRIVASTAVA

DEDICATION

This book is dedicated to my mother, Mrs. Manju Verma, my father, Mr. Hemant Kumar Verma, my mother-in-law, late Sindhu Srivastava, and my father-in-law, Dr. Ashok Kumar Srivastava.

CONTENTS

Chapter 7: Empowering Communities and Individuals in Circular Practices 129

Chapter 8: Measuring and Tracking Circular Economy Impact 145

Chapter 9: Overcoming Challenges in the Circular Transition 157

Chapter 10: Vision for a Circular Future 173

PREFACE

Dear Reader,

As we face urgent challenges like environmental damage and economic inequality, it is clear that the way we define prosperity needs to change. *"Redesigning Prosperity: From Waste to Wealth – A Blueprint for Sustainable Progress"* is my attempt to offer a new perspective on how we can build a future that's both sustainable and fair for everyone.

This book is about the circular economy—a way of thinking and doing things that break away from the traditional "take-make-waste" approach. Instead, it is about rethinking how we use resources, reducing waste, and finding ways to create lasting value. It is a practical guide meant for everyone: policymakers, business leaders, academics, students, and everyday people who want to be part of the change.

Throughout the chapters, I take you on a journey. We start by understanding the core ideas behind the circular economy and why they matter today more than ever. From there, we explore stories of real people, businesses, and communities that have embraced this model, showing us that sustainability and innovation can go hand in hand.

As we move deeper into the book, I share strategies, frameworks, and tools for putting circular principles into practice. These chapters are designed to give policymakers insights into how they can create policies that encourage circularity, and they offer businesses practical advice on how to adopt sustainable practices. For the academic community, I provide a thoughtful look at the theory behind these ideas, backed by research and case studies.

One of the things I have worked hard to do in this book is make it accessible. Whether you are an expert or just starting to learn about sustainability, I want you to feel engaged and inspired. **I have taken care to explain ideas in a way that makes sense for anyone—from busy professionals who need quick, actionable insights to policymakers looking for real-world solutions to everyday people who want to make small but meaningful changes in their lives.**

This book draws from my academic work, professional experiences, and personal passion for sustainability. I hope that Redesigning Prosperity will encourage you to think differently about success—not as endless consumption but as creating systems that support people and the planet.

Together, let's embrace the idea of Redesigning Prosperity, shifting our focus from short-term gains to long-term sustainability, and building a world that thrives for generations to come.

I am thrilled to join you on this transformative journey. As we explore shifting from a linear to a circular economy for a brighter future, I look forward to being your companion.

I am confident that the insights you will gather from this book will equip you to become a champion of sustainable development.

May your reading experience be both illuminating and rewarding.

Regards,
Dr. Meenakshi Srivastava

FOREWORD

In today's complex and interconnected world, where climate change, resource scarcity, and social inequality are no longer distant threats but daily realities, the very meaning of prosperity is being questioned. For decades, corporate success was measured by profits, scale, and market dominance. But the tides are turning. More than ever, businesses, policymakers, and individuals are being called upon to contribute to a deeper, more lasting form of value—one that sustains not just balance sheets but the planet and its people.

As Client Partner of a company that is actively striving to embed sustainability into the core of our operations and also offering these services to our esteemed clientle, I have witnessed firsthand the power of circular thinking. The transition from a linear "take-make-dispose" model to one that regenerates and reuses has not only been good for the environment—it has driven innovation, increased resilience, and unlocked new forms of value creation. Yet, this transition is not easy. It requires a fundamental shift in mindset, operations, and purpose.

This is where Redesigning Prosperity – A Blueprint for Sustainable Progress plays a vital role.

I have known Dr. Meenakshi for ages, a doting wife, caring mother, and very soft-spoken but extremely determined and passionate about her studies, responsibilities, and sustainability. She has masterfully woven together compelling stories, insightful analysis, and practical strategies to illuminate the path toward a circular economy. This book doesn't just highlight the problems—it offers solutions. It doesn't simply criticize outdated models—it reimagines what prosperity can and should look like in the 21st century. It provides a clear and inspiring roadmap for professionals, entrepreneurs, educators, and changemakers alike who are ready to become part of the solution.

One of the most powerful elements of this book is its accessibility. Whether you're a seasoned sustainability professional or someone just beginning to explore how your choices impact the world, you'll find ideas here that spark action. The real-world case studies, transformative principles, and step-by-step insights make this book a valuable companion for anyone who wants to build a future where economic growth does not come at the expense of ecological or human well-being.

I am proud to endorse this work because I believe it speaks to the conscience of modern business and society. It reminds us that the legacy we leave behind will be defined not by how much we extracted but by how well we created, reused, and restored.

As you turn these pages, I invite you to read not just with your intellect but with your intention. The future of prosperity is not written yet—it is waiting to be redesigned.

PK [Priyaranjan Kumar]
AVP & Client Partner - India
Cognizant Technology Solutions

INTRODUCTION: THE NEED TO REDESIGN PROSPERITY

"If you want to change the world for a better place to live in,

First of all, you will change in yourself and all around you."

What does prosperity mean to you? For centuries, it has been tied to economic growth, material wealth, and consumption. These ideas have driven progress and improved lives, but they have also come at a steep cost—environmental damage, resource depletion, and rising inequality. As we face the challenges of a changing climate and dwindling resources, it is time to rethink prosperity.

The problem is not with prosperity itself but with how we have pursued it. Our current economic systems operate on a linear model: take resources, make products, and discard waste. While this approach has fuelled growth, it has left mountains of waste, polluted environments, and stressed ecosystems behind. This model is no longer sustainable. We need a fresh perspective that balances economic success with environmental and social well-being.

The solution lies in Redesigning Prosperity. Imagine an economy where resources are reused, waste becomes an opportunity, and innovation drives sustainability. This is the essence of the circular economy. It is not about giving up what we value but about using resources smarter, creating systems that regenerate, and redefining how we measure success.

This book explores how we can shift from "take-make-waste" to a more resilient and inclusive system. It is a call to action to embrace new ideas, challenge old norms, and envision a future where prosperity and sustainability go hand in hand.

Before going further, I want to share a small story:

The Wise Farmer's Legacy

In a quiet village, there lived an old farmer named Raghav. He had worked tirelessly on his land, growing enough crops to feed his family and sell in the market. His neighbours admired his wealth, but what made him truly wise was his long-term thinking.

One day, his son, Arjun, asked, *"Father, why don't we sell all the harvest and enjoy a grand feast every season? Why do you always store grains and save money instead?"*

Raghav smiled and took Arjun to a giant mango tree near their farm. *"Do you see this tree?"* he asked. *"My grandfather planted it when he was young. He never enjoyed its fruits, but today, we do. Just as he left this tree for us, we must leave something for the next generation."*

He continued, *"If we consume everything today, what will be left for tomorrow? We must not only meet our needs but also think of our children's future. This is why I store grains, save money, and invest in our land. It ensures that you and your children will always have enough, even in difficult times."*

Years later, when Raghav passed away, Arjun followed his father's wisdom. He expanded the farm, planted more trees, and saved wisely. His children grew up in prosperity, just as his father had intended.

The story reminds us that true prosperity isn't just about fulfilling our present desires—it's about ensuring a secure and sustainable future for the generations to come.

According to the Brundtland Report, "sustainable development is a development that fulfills the needs of the present without compromising the ability of future generations to meet their own needs".

From the above story and the definition of sustainable development, it is quite clear that **for making sustainable progress it is important to redesign prosperity, and we can achieve it only through circular economy.**

Let us delve deeply into the need to redesign prosperity:

Sustainability Challenge

We live in a world, which is at a critical juncture. The approach, which is used for improvement, is rooted in traditional growth models and has brought significant advancements but left a trail of ecological devastation, social inequality, and economic instability. Now, it is time to think about a machine that is running at full capacity and utilising scarce resources without pause; as a result, sooner or later, it not only overheats and stops working but also breaks down. Today, we stand on the same path and staring at the consequences of a linear economy that prioritises short-term gains over long-term sustainability.

Traditional growth models face various environmental and economic challenges.

The Environmental Crisis

The scars of our unchecked consumption are etched into the Earth's surface. Forests are shrinking, oceans are choked with plastic, and biodiversity is unprecedentedly vanishing. The UN estimates that if current trends continue, humanity will need the resources of three planets to sustain itself by 2050. Rising temperatures, melting glaciers, and extreme weather events are not merely distant warnings but are today's reality.

Let us take the example of the Great Pacific Garbage Patch, a swirling mass of plastic waste twice the size of Texas. It is not just an environmental nightmare but a stark symbol of how our "take, use, dispose" culture is unsustainable.

Economic Instability in a Finite World

Linear growth models are also economically unstable. Industries reliant on finite resources face escalating costs, that interrupt supply chains and give uncertain futures. The 2021 semiconductor shortage crippled sectors like automotive and electronics, illustrating that our extractive systems are how much vulnerable.

Even on an individual level, the cracks are visible. Not only do families struggle with rising living costs, but businesses also face unpredictable raw material prices, and governments are burdened with escalating waste management challenges.

Social Inequities and Health Hazards

The human toll of this model is devastating. Polluted air, contaminated water, and unsafe working conditions disproportionately affect marginalised communities. The WHO estimates that air pollution alone causes 7 million premature deaths annually. Can we continue to call this "progress" when it costs lives and leaves future generations with a compromised planet?

Why Redesign Prosperity?

This book is not just about the problems but about the solutions. It is a call to rethink our approach to growth and prosperity—a shift from the linear, extractive model to a regenerative, *circular economy*. As you turn these pages, you will explore how innovation, collaboration, and values-driven practices can create a future where economic growth and sustainability coexist.

Let this chapter be the spark that lights a fire of curiosity and determination. The path ahead is not easy, but it is necessary. Together, let's reimagine prosperity—not as something we take from the planet but as something we create in harmony with it.

Why Circularity: The Promise of a Regenerative Economy

Suppose a bustling marketplace, where each product, from the simplest to the most advanced gadget, carries a hidden cost, which is nothing else but a trail of scrap and waste of resources. The reason for this is the traditional economic model. Now, consider a world where that waste simply does not exist, where each and every product becomes the building block for something new once its initial purpose is fulfilled. This is nothing other than the vision of a circular economy. The shift is so transformative it redefines not only how we consume but also how we thrive.

Breaking Free from the Wasteful Linear Model

For decades, our economic systems have followed a linear path: take, make, use, and throw away. This "use and discard" culture has brought us on the verge of economic and ecological collapse. The mountains of landfills overflowing with non-biodegradable plastics, e-waste in developing countries, and oceans filled with microplastics are not just statistics; **they are symptoms of a model that has outlived its utility.**

But what would happen if we broke this cycle? What will happen if the end of one product's life marks the beginning of another's? This possibility is offered only by the circular economy.

What is Circularity?

Now, this is an important question: what is circularity?

At its core, **circularity challenges us to design products, systems, and processes that entirely eliminate waste. It is nothing but shifting from extraction and disposal to regeneration and renewal.** Imagine a lightbulb designed in such a way that it can be not only fully disassembled but also reused or a pair of sneakers made entirely from biodegradable materials. Circularity is not just about recycling, but it is rethinking the entire lifecycle of a product.

A Regenerative Path Forward

Real-world examples demonstrate the potential for change. In the Netherlands, corporations such as Philips are leading the way with innovative "product-as-a-service" approaches, offering appliance leases rather than outright sales. This strategy ensures that products are returned, refurbished, and reused. Meanwhile, in Sweden, repair cafes are empowering individuals to mend broken items, ranging from clothes to electronic devices, giving new life to objects that might otherwise end up as waste.

More than Just an Economic Shift

This shift is more than just an economic shift because after sailing from a linear to a circular economy, we will understand how this is important for present and future generations. So, now it has become a requirement of time.

The circular economy is not just an environmental necessity but also an economic opportunity. Studies show it could generate $4.5 trillion in global economic benefits by 2030 through efficient resource use, reduced waste, and job creation in green industries. It is also a cultural reset that reminds us that prosperity does not have to come at the expense of the planet.

As you delve deeper into this book, you will discover how circularity is not just an idea but a roadmap—a roadmap that promises a world where waste becomes wealth, **and our economy serves both people and the planet.** Let's uncover the endless possibilities of thinking in circles.

What to Expect in This Book: A Blueprint for Sustainable Progress

As you embark on this journey through *Redesigning Prosperity*, you are not just reading a book but stepping into a movement. This book is designed to be more than a collection of ideas; it is a practical guide, an inspiration, and a call to action. It is for anyone who dreams of a world where economic growth no longer costs the Earth and where resilient communities, thriving businesses, and a healthy planet coexist.

A Practical Blueprint for Change

This book breaks down the principles of the circular economy into actionable insights, offering individuals and organisations a clear path forward. From understanding the fundamental flaws of our current systems to exploring innovative solutions, each chapter equips you with tools to create meaningful change. **Whether you are a policymaker, business leader, academic, student, or environmentally conscious individual, you will find strategies tailored to your role in the circular transition.**

What You'll Discover

- **Inspiration Through Stories**: Dive into real-world case studies like IKEA's waste reduction efforts and Dell's closed-loop recycling systems. These success stories prove that circularity is not just possible but also, profitable and scalable.
- **Actionable Solutions**: Learn practical ways how to implement circular principles in your own life and

work, that is, from hosting repair cafes to designing products with regenerative lifecycles.

- **The Role of Innovation and Technology**: Understand how advancements in material science, AI, and blockchain are transforming the way we recycle, track, and optimise resources.

- **Overcoming Challenges**: Explore strategies to tackle economic costs, cultural resistance, and regulatory barriers with creative solutions like partnerships, consumer education, and awareness.

Now, it is time to transform yourself for sustainability. It is not only enough to know what to do for circular practices. You also need to understand the importance of and the methodology for removing linear practices and habits that are holding you back. I will also make you understand how to transform your linear practices and develop valuable success habits of circular practices that will change your life forever.

A Vision of a Better Future

In each chapter, you will find and understand glimpses of what is possible. That includes green factories producing zero waste, flourishing cities powered by renewable energy, and communities adopting a "waste is wealth" mindset. **This book does not just ask you to imagine a better world, it also shows you how to help build it.** Let this book be your companion and guide, igniting hope and determination as you turn the pages. Together, we will explore how circular principles can lead us to a future where prosperity aligns with sustainability, which is a future worth striving for.

How to Read This Book

As you are reading, I strongly encourage you to underline and highlight everything that feels important to you. Make notes in the margin about the things you will put into action. Then, review these notes and highlight the section again and again. Repetition is the key to real learning. Every time you reread portions of this book, you will literally "re-mind" yourself what you need to do to get from where you are to where you want to be. As you will discover, it takes repetitive exposure to a new idea before it becomes a natural part of your thinking and being.

You may also discover that you are already familiar with some of the principles here. That is great! But ask yourself, am I currently practicing them? If not, make a commitment to put them into action—now!

You might find it useful to connect with one or two other people who would like to join you as accountability partners to ensure that each of you actually implements what you learn. True learning only occurs when you assimilate and apply the new information—when there is a change in your behaviour.

Of course, any change requires sustained effort to overcome years' worth of internal and external resistance. It is natural to encounter obstacles and feel temporarily stuck on a plateau when achieving any goal. This is normal. Be patient. Hang in there. Do not give up. You will break through.

Okay, let's get started.

1

THE JOURNEY FROM LINEAR TO CIRCULAR ECONOMIES

"The greatest threat to our planet is the belief that someone else will save it."
— Robert Swan

"The greatest solutions often lie not in resisting change, but in redefining it. Shifting from linear to circular is not just a choice—it's a solution for a sustainable future."

Can we rethink what prosperity truly means? Imagine a world where growth does not harm the planet but instead works in harmony with it—where waste becomes a valuable resource, and progress is sustainable. This vision lies at the heart of transitioning from a linear to a circular economy—a shift that changes how we use resources, design products, and imagine the future.

For too long, we have followed a "take-make-waste" system: taking resources, making products, and tossing them aside as waste without thinking about tomorrow. This approach fuelled economic growth but left us with overflowing landfills, disappearing resources, and a planet in crisis. It is clear—we cannot keep going like this.

But here is the good news: we can do better. A circular economy offers a brighter path. It is about designing products to last, using resources wisely, and finding new value in what we used to call waste. It is built on simple but powerful ideas: reuse, repair, and recycle. Instead of depleting the planet, it is about regenerating it.

This chapter explores how adopting a circular mindset can protect the environment, build a stronger economy, and improve lives. It is more than just an economic shift—it is a change in how we think about progress and prosperity, reminding us to care for the world we live in.

The linear model treats precious resources like water, minerals, and fossil fuels as if they will never run out, leading to overuse and destruction. Products are made quickly, with little thought for how they will last or where they will end up.

The result? Oceans are full of plastic, ecosystems are under threat, and the planet is struggling to keep up.

But it does not have to be this way. **We can create a future where resources are respected, waste is transformed, and prosperity is reimagined—for ourselves and the generations to come.**

Linear Economy: The "Take-Make-Waste" Model

Picture an endless conveyor system beginning in a verdant woodland, traversing through industrial and city environments, and terminating at an enormous waste site. This system represents the core of the linear economy, a straightforward path where natural resources are harvested, converted into goods, and eventually thrown away. This framework's progression is one-way, resulting in colossal heaps of refuse and exhausted natural assets.

The linear economic model treats resources like minerals, water, and fossil fuels as infinite. We extract, fell, bore, and harvest often without regard for sustainability. Following this exploitation phase is production, which converts raw materials into consumer products, emphasising speed and volume over longevity and recyclability. Once these items become obsolete, they enter the disposal phase, joining countless tonnes of discarded goods that damage ecosystems and contaminate our seas.

Sketch:

The following sketches clearly illustrate the functioning of a linear economy, depicting its process and ultimate contribution to landfill.

1)

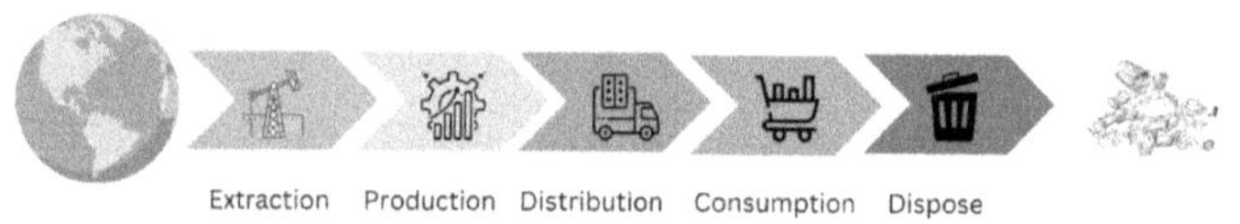

2)

Emotional costs are steep: After discarding the smartphone, the old appliances or plastic bottles became lost resources that could have been reused. Each item represents an opportunity to construct a more sustainable future. **Over the years, this take-make-waste approach has fuelled resource scarcity, environmental degradation, and climate instability, pushing the planet closer to a point at which an ecosystem can no longer cope with environmental change and the ecosystem suddenly shifts from one state to another, which is called the ecological tipping point.**

Let us consider the example of a simple plastic bottle: Extracting petroleum, the main ingredient depletes fossil fuels. It emits CO_2 and uses energy during manufacturing, which results in pollution. The bottle takes up to 450 years to decompose in a landfill, and after discarding it, it can end up in the ocean, harming marine life. **Each bottle is a small example of a massive unsustainable system.**

Interactive Prompt for Readers: Think about a product you have used today that is single-use. Could it be replaced by something more sustainable or avoided? Take a second to note what change you could make tomorrow, using a reusable bag or a refillable bottle.

Impact: Globally, a linear economy exhausts resources faster than it can refill: Rivers dry up, forests shrink, and entire species are lost because Earth struggles to keep up with patterns of its consumption. To change direction, it is important to understand the profound impacts of this model and recognise that a different approach, one that values regeneration and longevity, is not only possible but essential for sustainability.

Circular Economy

Consider Earth as a sealed vault of resources. In a circular economic model, nothing leaves this vault; all the materials are repurposed, restored, or regenerated. This concept starkly contrasts the traditional linear "extract-produce-discard" model, in which resources are permanently lost. **The circular economy is built on five fundamental principles: reduce, reuse, recycle, reimagine, and regenerate, each serving as a safeguard to preserve the resource vault for the upcoming generations.**

Sketch:

The following sketch illustrates a circular economy's fundamental principles, depicting zero waste.

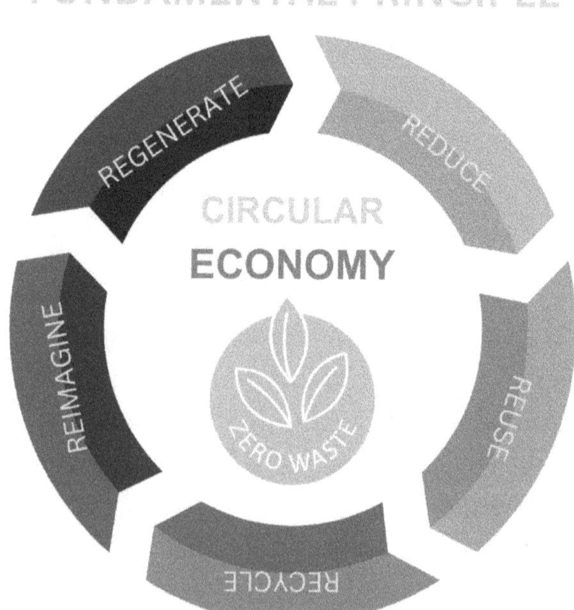

1. Reduce

Consider this approach as "conscious reduction." **The process of decreasing consumption begins with efficiency: utilising fewer resources and energy to fulfil the same requirements.** For example, swapping disposable plastics for long-lasting alternatives such as bamboo utensils decreases waste at its origin. Reduction is not solely about deprivation; it is about making wiser decisions that generate enduring worth.

2. Reuse

Repurposing items is comparable to inheriting cherished family possessions. **Well-crafted products have the potential for multiple applications.** Consider the example of glass containers in India, which are often utilised several times before being processed for recycling. Reusing items create sentimental attachments, evoking memories of an era in which durability is prioritised over disposability.

3. Recycle

Recycling serves as a crucial safeguard in a circular economy. Unlike the traditional linear model in which materials are discarded after use, recycling ensures that resources are reintroduced into the system. A prime example is aluminium cans, which can undergo endless recycling without quality degradation. This process conserves up to 95% of the energy required to produce new aluminium from raw materials.

4. Redesign

The concept revolves around innovative thinking. Consider a T-shirt engineered to break down into a natural fertiliser or an automobile constructed for simple disassembly and component reuse. Trailblazing companies such as Patagonia are creating products with longevity and ease of repair. Innovation and environmental consciousness intersect in the realm of redesign

5. Regenerate

In this regard, the natural world serves as the greatest instructor. **Similar to how forests regenerate after shedding their foliage, restorative practices help to revitalise ecosystems.** One example is regenerative farming, which rejuvenates soil health, thereby promoting biodiversity and increasing carbon sequestration.

Contrast with Linear Practices

Linear practices treat resources as disposable; circular principles treat them as renewable. Where linear systems exhaust, circular systems replenish. **Where waste is the endpoint in linear models, it is the starting point in circular ones.**

Interactive Prompt for Readers:

Think about the life cycle of an everyday item like a coffee cup under both linear and circular models. How does its journey differ? For example: In the linear model, it is used once and discarded; in the circular model, it is designed for reuse or biodegradable.

Sketch:

The following sketches clearly illustrate the functioning of a circular economy, depicting its process and ultimate contribution to zero waste.

1)

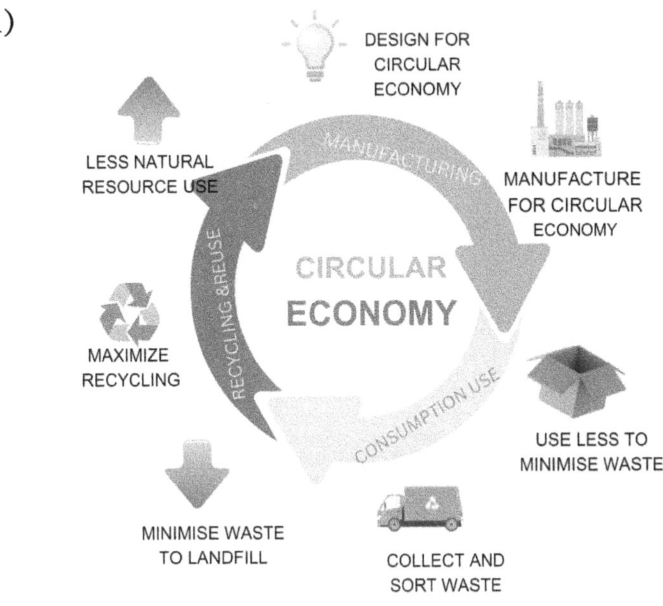

2)

The above two-part diagram shows, on the left, a straight line showing a tree (resource) turning into a paper cup (product) and ending in a landfill (waste). On the right, a loop shows the same tree leading to a compostable cup, decomposing into the soil, and nourishing another tree.

Practical Scenario:

The following picture shows the power of a circular economy:

Here is a picture of a city adopting circular systems: residents use community compost bins, businesses offer electronics repair stations, and government incentives support startups creating products from recycled materials. Now imagine the air cleaner, resources richer, and people prouder of their contributions.

It is the power of the circular economy that invites us to be stewards, and make sure that the treasure chest of Earth remains full for all generations.

Case for Change

Why Is the Circular Model Essential for Long-Term Prosperity? This can be easily understood by remembering Aesop's fable of the goose and the golden egg.

This fable is the story of a poor farmer who one day discovers in the nest of his pet goose a glittering golden egg. At first, he thinks it must be some kind of trick. But as he starts to throw the egg aside, he has second thoughts and takes it in to be appraised instead.

The egg is pure gold! The farmer cannot believe his good fortune. He becomes even more incredulous the following day when the experience is repeated. Day after day, he awakens to rush to the nest and find another golden egg. He becomes fabulously wealthy; it all seems too good to be true.

But with his increasing comes greed and impatience. Unable to wait day after day for the golden eggs, the farmer decides he will kill the goose and get them all at once. But when he opens, he finds it empty. There are no golden eggs—and there is no way to get any more. The farmer has destroyed the goose that produced them.

I suggest that within this fable is a natural law, a principle—the basic definition of effectiveness. Most people see effectiveness from the golden egg paradigm: the more you produce, the more you do, and the more effective you are.

However, as the story shows, true effectiveness is the function of what is produced (the golden eggs) and the producing asset or capacity to produce (the goose).

> If you adopt a pattern of life that focuses on golden eggs and neglects the goose, you will soon be without the asset that produces golden eggs. On the other hand, if you only take care of the goose with no aim towards golden eggs, you soon will not have the wherewithal to feed yourself or the goose.
>
> Effectiveness lies in the balance of production of desired results and production capability.

Picture Earth as a golden goose, capable of providing for humanity indefinitely—if treated with care. But the linear economy treats it like an endless ATM, withdrawing resources without replenishment. With time, the goose weakens, its eggs become fewer, and the cycle collapses. The circular economy provides a lifeline to protect this goose, and long-term prosperity and stability will be ensured.

The Urgency for Change

Linear practices are not sustainable. The **World Bank estimates global waste will grow by 70% by 2050** if urgent action is not taken. Meanwhile, resources such as water, minerals, and arable land are depleting at alarming rates. This model of "take-make-waste" not only endangers natural ecosystems but also exacerbates social inequalities and economic instability. **Without a shift from Linear to Circular, future generations risk inheriting a depleted, unstable world.**

The Circular Advantage

The circular model focuses attention on regeneration over-exploitation, creating a foundation that is for lasting prosperity. These are some advantages that we get after practicing the circular model.

1. **Economic Stability: Circular practices give Economic Stability with reducing dependence on finite resources, stabilising supply chains, and mitigating price shocks.**

   a. **Example:** During shortages of global semiconductors, companies with recycling programmes go through fewer disruptions.

2. **Environmental Restoration: Circular practices provide Environmental Restoration by minimising waste and encouraging regeneration. The circular model combats climate change, promotes biodiversity, and restores ecosystems.**

   a. **Fact:** Techniques of Circular agriculture can enhance soil health and boost yields by up to 40%.

   b. As per the Circularity Gap Report 2021, presented by the World Economic Forum, the implementation of a circular economy model can cut global greenhouse gas emission by 39%.

   c. As per Ellen Macarthur Foundation Report a completely circular economy, along with industrial symbiosis, may cause 32% decline in primary material usage by 2030 and a 53% decline by 2050.

3. **Social Equity:** Circular practices help to provide **Social Equity. Circular systems create local jobs in repair, recycling, and redesign.** Circular systems promote economic inclusivity and resilience.

Emotional Appeal

Think of a family heirloom, which passed down generations. Its value grow not because it is new but because it endures. Now, it is the time to treat resources with similar reverence. The circular economy allows humanity to value durability and renewal over disposability. It is not just about saving the planet; it is about honouring our shared legacy.

Interactive Prompt

Now, it is time to think about your daily habits: What disposable items could you replace with reusable alternatives? Note down one change you will make this week—such as repurposing old clothing or switching to a refillable water bottle.

Practical Scenario

Envisioning a city transformed by circular systems, where the following practices are going on --

- Local governments help turn organic waste into fertiliser and incentivise composting.
- Startups create products that is innovative such as shoes made from ocean plastic.
- Community workshops teach rebuild skills, empowering individuals to fix instead of discard.

What is the result? Thriving ecosystems, cleaner air, and empowered citizens proud to contribute a future that is regenerative.

Which we want. That is not only our desire, but essential for survival.

Sketch:

1) The Following Picture shows Linear Economy vs. circular Economy:

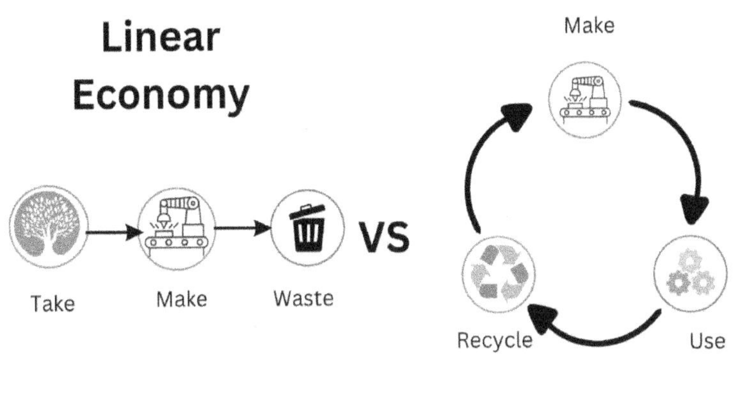

2) The Following split Image shows impact of Linear Economy and Circular Economy:

Image shows: left side, a barren landscape showing the toll of linear economy. & right side, a sustainable city with circular practices in action— compost bins, repair shops, recycling hubs, and collective gardens.

The circular model is more than a choice—it is a responsibility. It is the blueprint for a future where prosperity and stability are not fleeting, but enduring.

Recap and Summary:

1. Linear Economy and its impact:

The linear economy works on a "take-make-waste" model, where resources are taken, made into products, and thrown away as waste after use. This approach is unsustainable, because of that, natural resources are depleted, excessive waste is generated, and that harms ecosystems. It fails to deal with long-term economic and social stability, and creates an urgency for change

2. Introducing the Circular Economy:

The circular economy is a model that works on regenerative. Its foundation works on principles such as consumption being reduced, materials being reused, products being recycled, systems being redesigned, and resources being regenerated.

3. Key Principles of Circularity:

   a. **Reduce:** Minimise resource waste and extraction.
   b. **Reuse:** Increase the product utility.
   c. **Recycle:** Waste transforms into raw materials.

d.   **Redesign**: Innovation for sustainability.
e.   **Regenerate**: Natural ecosystems be restored.

4. Contrast Between Models:

In a linear economy, resources are treated as disposable, leading to waste and depletion. In contrast, in the circular economy, resources are treated as renewable, emphasising a continuous regeneration cycle.

5. The Case for Change:

Transitioning to a circular model is important for handling global challenges such as waste management, resource scarcity, and climate change. It guarantees environmental sustainability, economic stability, and social equity.

6. Real-World Examples:

Sweden's ReTuna mall shows how upcycling and recycling can create sustainable and profitable business models.

7. Interactive Reflections:

Readers must evaluate their consumption habits, consider sustainable alternatives, and envision a world where products are designed for renewal and longevity.

8. The Vision Ahead:

The journey from linear to circular is about Redesigning Prosperity—ensuring that economic growth is aligned with ecological balance and societal well-being for future generations.

Closing Thought:

The shift from a linear to a circular economy is not just a trend; it is a transformative movement. By embracing this journey, we will achieve the future that is important for survival. Now, it is time to redefine prosperity as not just wealth but a sustainable legacy for the planet and humanity.

2

BUILDING BLOCKS OF THE CIRCULAR ECONOMY

"Waste is a design flaw."

— Kate Kreba, Sustainability Expert

"We do not inherit the Earth from our ancestors; we borrow it from our children."

— Native American Proverb

Imagine the construction of a house intended to last generations. The strength of its foundation determines its resilience. **The circular economy works on a similar concept; its success lies in its foundational elements—efficient use of resources, innovative designs, and systems that ensure nothing goes to waste.** This chapter delves deep into these important building blocks, exploring how they transform industries and societies. From sustainable design to circular business models, these components give us the power to create an economy that thrives without harming the planet. Together, they form the blueprint for a future where prosperity and sustainability walk hand in hand.

Essential Elements

Well, what are the Core Components of Circularity?

When constructing a house, we think about the material we use and how it is used because it is not built only for the present generation. We may say that each brick is carefully chosen to be reshaped, reused, or restored if a house is built to stand for generations. The circular economy works in the same way as in this timeless house. **The circular economy depends on three essential pillars: sustainable design, resource efficiency, and closed-loop systems.** These foundational elements ensure that prosperity flourishes without exhausting the planet's resources.

1. Sustainable Design: Building for Durability and Renewal

Sustainable design is the blueprint of circularity, in which products are composed of foresight and intention. **These** items are designed to last, be repaired, or transform into something new that does not resemble a disposable good.

- **Example:** Adidas' "Futurecraft Loop" sneakers are a good example of sustainable design. It is made entirely from recyclable materials, designed to be disassembled and remanufactured into new shoes.
- **Metaphor:** It is just like composing a seed that grows into a tree, sheds its leaves to make the soil more fertile, and continues the cycle.

2. Resource Efficiency: Maximising Every Ounce of Value

What is the meaning of maximising every ounce of value? Yes, it is right that you understood. We must use our resources in such a way, just like that Honeybee sucks all the pollen from flowers. But after that, do not throw it as waste but try to give it new life.

Resource efficiency is defined as producing more economic value with less resource input. It is a practice in which producers aim to get maximum output from resources while producing minimum waste.

Resource efficiency is all about doing more with less, extracting the maximum value from resources while minimising waste.

> - **Fact:** The Ellen MacArthur Foundation reports that optimising material use or resource efficiency in industries like construction could save $1 trillion annually by 2030.

- **Practical Scenario**: Imagine a café that uses spent coffee grounds to make compost or even beauty products, turning a byproduct into a valuable resource.

3. Closed-Loop Systems: Keeping Resources in Motion

Keeping resources in motion is a beautiful concept; without it, we cannot think of a circular economy. This differentiates between linear and circular economies. The closed-loop system talks about using anything, not throwing it as waste but giving it another life after redesigning or remanufacturing.

Closed-loop systems ensure that materials and products flow continuously through the economy rather than end up in landfills. It is a processing system in which effluents are recycled, treated, and returned for reuse.

Case Study: Tesla's Gigafactory and its Closed-Loop System

Initially, Tesla faced the challenge of securing a sustainable supply chain for lithium-ion batteries, which was crucial for their electric vehicles (EVs). The production of these batteries heavily depends on mining raw materials, such as lithium, cobalt, and nickel, which pose ethical and environmental concerns. Recognising this, Tesla has started investing in recycling technologies as part of its Gigafactory operations.

Tesla partnered with specialised recycling companies and developed in-house systems to recover materials from used batteries. They implemented processes to efficiently extract valuable elements such as lithium, cobalt, and nickel. To monitor progress, Tesla incorporated a system to track material recovery rates and established standards for sustainability improvement.

Tesla achieved significant milestones after maturing the closed-loop system. Recycled materials were reintegrated into new batteries, lowering production costs, reducing reliance on mining, and minimising environmental impact. This initiative set a precedent in the EV industry, highlighting the potential of circular economic practices for sustainable innovation.

Interactive Prompt:

Now, it is time to think about your daily waste. Which items are part of the closed-loop system? Could your plastic bottle be turned into a park bench? Make a list of such items:

____

____

____

____

____

____

____

Sketch:

Visualise the three elements in a triangular diagram:

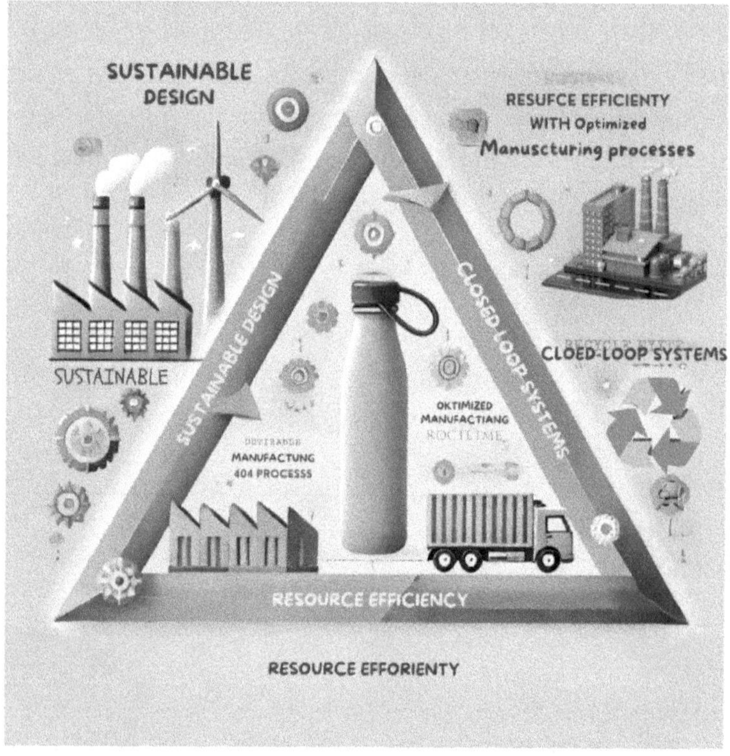

- One side depicts sustainable design with a durable, repairable product.
- Another side illustrates resource efficiency, such as optimised manufacturing processes.
- The final side shows closed-loop systems, like a recycling chain.

These building blocks are essential and interconnected conditions for an effective circular economy. **It teaches us to consider waste not as an end but as a new beginning,** reminding us that, such as the house built to last, the sustainability requirement is thoughtful foundations.

Circular Economy Models: Key Business Innovations

Thus, what key business innovations provide the right direction for a circular economy? Now, it is time to ponder it.

Imagine a river flowing endlessly, nourishing the landscape while never exhausting itself. Circular economy business models imitate this flow and are designed to circulate value continuously without depleting resources. But how is it possible? It is possible only by using fewer resources in a way that fulfils the needs of the whole economy. The following are **three transformative models of a circular economy.** These are **Product-as-a-Service, the sharing economy, and remanufacturing.**

1. Product-as-a-Service (PaaS): Owning Value, Not Things

Suppose we use a water purifier for the lease. So, we can call the company and act accordingly when there is any difficulty. In other words, if repair is required, they do so. Otherwise taken back by them and instead throwing it as a waste, they renovate and remanufactured or reuse it

In the PaaS model of a circular economy, the focus shifts from ownership to access. Companies retain ownership and lease it to customers instead of selling products. This model ensures longevity and reuse.

- **Example:** Let us take Philips's example, which offers lighting as a service where customers pay for light rather than bulbs. Philips was responsible for maintenance and recycling, creating a closed-loop system.

- **Metaphor**: Think of a symphony where the music itself remains timeless and reusable, but you rent the music sheet, using it to create harmony.
- **Interactive Idea**: Now, it is time for you to answer and consider what products in your lives—like electronics or furniture—could be rented instead of owned. For me, it is a water purifier and light. And what is for you? Make a list:

____

____

____

____

____

____

2. The Sharing Economy: Maximising Utilisation

How should we maximise utilisation? Suppose that we live in a large joint family. Many items are not used daily, but they are used according to need, e.g., a toolbox. Therefore, we make a place for that type of thing, and all family members use it on time. However, we now live in small families. Therefore, we think that it is for a group or society. This concept is a sharing economy.

The sharing economy is an economic model in which goods and resources are shared by individuals and groups in a collaborative manner, such that physical assets become services. The sharing economy encourages the communal use of resources and reduces idle capacity and waste.

- **Example:** Companies such as Airbnb and Uber, which maximise existing resources (homes and cars) rather than creating new ones, are good examples of a sharing economy.

Airbnb is a prime example of the sharing economy, using existing homes rather than requiring new construction. This approach fosters resource efficiency, allowing homeowners to earn extra income while providing travellers with unique lodging options. On the societal front, it boosts local economies by increasing tourism and supporting small businesses.

Uber is also a good example of the sharing economy. It connects people who need rides with drivers who already own cars, making better use of existing resources than adding new ones. This model provides job opportunities, improves transportation accessibility, and reduces the need for personal car ownership.

> - **Fact:** It is a fact that a shared car can replace up to 15 privately owned vehicles, significantly reducing resource use and emissions.

- **Practical Scenario:** Imagine a tool library neighbourhood where residents borrow seldom-used items such as drills or ladders, saving money and space while reducing production demand.

Are you ready for the sharing economy?

3. Remanufacturing: Breathing New Life into Products

Suppose about your favourite dress, that you like most. Unfortunately, one day after washing, it was torn in such a way that it was not used. After thinking so much about it, you think you should redesign it and make it new with the help of other materials. You did it, and after that, you used stylish. Yes, right, which is the concept from which we are going to interact with remanufacturing.

Remanufacturing is the rebuilding of a product according to the specifications of the original manufactured product using a combination of reused, repaired, and new parts. This is the industrial process of returning used products to a new or better condition, extending their lifecycle, and reducing the need for raw materials.

Case Study: Caterpillar's Remanufacturing for Sustainability and Savings

Caterpillar initially faced a challenge: how to provide cost-effective solutions for heavy machinery maintenance while addressing environmental concerns. The traditional approach of manufacturing new parts was expensive and resource-intensive, leading to significant waste and a higher carbon footprint.

To address this issue, Caterpillar introduced a remanufacturing programme. They began collecting used machinery parts and restoring them to new conditions by using advanced technologies and rigorous quality checks. Over time, they refined the process, ensuring that the remanufactured parts met the same performance standards as the new ones. To monitor success, Caterpillar has implemented systems to track customer satisfaction, cost savings, and environmental benefits.

These results were transformative. Customers benefited from 40-70% more affordable parts, while Caterpillar significantly reduced raw material use and waste. This initiative not only enhanced customer loyalty but also showcased how circular economy practices can drive both profitability and sustainability.

- **Emotional Appeal**: Remanufacturing is similar to restoring a cherished antique chair, giving it a second life, and preserving its history.

Sketch:

Here is the three-panel illustration:

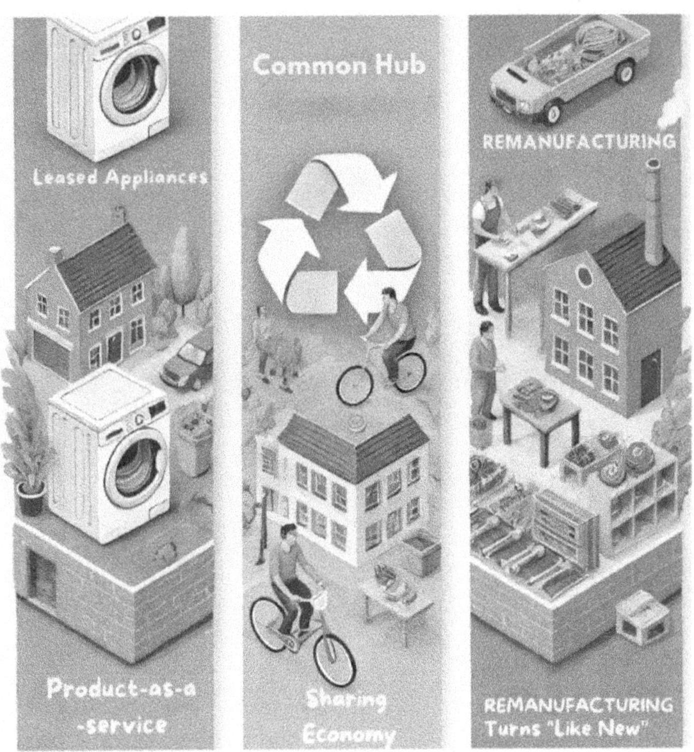

- **Panel 1:** A consumer using a leased appliance represent Product-as-a-Service (PaaS).

- **Panel 2**: A neighbourhood sharing tools and bikes from a common hub, illustrating the sharing economy.
- **Panel 3**: Workers refurbishing old machinery, turning "worn-out" products into "like new," representing remanufacturing.

Circular business models not only innovate but inspire also. They challenge us to rethink about the very concept of ownership. It is the pleasant question that is risen here "What if waste wasn't the end, but the beginning of something better?"

Impacts on Industries and Society

Imagine what happens after planting a tree: it grows taller and stronger over time, offering fruit, shade, and air for generations. Circular practices work on the same principle, and their ripple effect not only conserves resources but also profoundly transforms industries, economies, and societies.

The main impacts of a circular economy on industry and society are economic resilience, environmental healing, and social uplift. It is now time to explore this concept deeply.

1. Economic Resilience: Future-Proofing Industries

Developing a circular manufacturing economy makes extracting new resources less necessary. **The circular economy** paradigm aims to replace the linear take-make-waste production pattern and reduce the resources used and the waste generated. It **not only keeps products and materials in use for as long as possible but also recovers valuable materials and resources from waste, resulting** in decreased dependency on limited resources, making industries more flexible to supply chain disruptions and price volatility.

Case Study: Patagonia's "Worn Wear" Programme – Repairing for Sustainability and Loyalty

Patagonia has recognised a growing concern among eco-conscious consumers: the environmental impact of fast fashion. Initially, the focus was on creating durable products, but the brand saw an opportunity to go further by helping customers extend their clothing.

The "Worn Wear" programme offered free or low-cost repairs for damaged Patagonia gear. It began with mobile repair stations and expanded into an online platform for trade and second-hand purchase. The programme grew steadily and was supported by skilled technicians and customer education on sustainable practices. Patagonia monitored its success by tracking its repair volumes, customer engagement, and resource savings.

This programme had a profound impact. This reduces waste, conserves resources, and strengthens customer trust. Patagonia saved materials and built a loyal community of consumers aligned with its sustainability values, setting a benchmark for eco-friendly business practices.

> - **Fact**: According to the World Economic Forum, a circular economy can generate $4.5 trillion in economic benefits by 2030.

2. Environmental Healing: Reversing Damage

The shift from linear to circular will have a marked impact on pollution, one of the greatest threats to global biodiversity. **Reusing and recycling products would slow the use of natural resources, reduce landscape and habitat disruption, and help limit biodiversity loss. Circular systems address critical environmental challenges by reducing waste and greenhouse gas (GHG) emissions.** Circular practices work on the environment, so healing ointments work on the wound.

- **Example**: Denmark's Kalundborg Eco-Industrial Park uses waste from one industry as a resource for another, cutting carbon emissions and minimising landfill use.
- **Emotional Element**: Imagine a river once choked with waste. Now, with the help of circular practices, it is running clean and clear, and its revival sparks hope in a once-despondent community.

3. Social Upliftment: Empowering Communities

The circular economy promotes concepts such as sharing, repairing, and collaborating. **Circular practices create new jobs and opportunities in remanufacturing, repair, and recycling industries.**

Community-based initiatives such as repair cafes, swap events, refilleries, and reuse programmes can strengthen social ties, build trust, and empower individuals.

Empowering Communities through circular practices results in Social Upliftment.

Case Study: India's Informal Recycling Sector – A Path to Sustainable Livelihoods

India's cities have long faced challenges with waste management as growing urban populations generate massive amounts of waste. Initially, the burden of recycling fell in the informal sector, which comprised millions of workers who collected, sorted, and processed recyclable materials. While their efforts prevented waste from overwhelming cities and provided essential income to marginalised communities, these workers often faced poor working conditions, low wages, and health risks.

Efforts to scale circular practices began with pilot programmes by NGOs, businesses, and government bodies. These initiatives aim to integrate informal workers into formal waste management systems, providing them with training, safety equipment, and fair wages. Monitoring systems have been introduced to track worker participation, income improvements, and waste diversion rates.

These results are promising. Formalising these jobs has enhanced safety, raised income, and improved the efficiency of the recycling processes. Moreover, it has strengthened the circular economy, turning waste into a resource, uplifting vulnerable communities, and creating a sustainable urban development model.

- **Interactive Prompt:** Now, readers think about a product they no longer use. Could a repair service employ someone to extend its life or recycle an item to support local jobs?

Sketch:

Here is a three-part illustration:

1. **Economic Resilience**: Factories use fewer resources and save costs.
2. **Environmental Healing**: A revitalised river with green surroundings.
3. **Social Upliftment**: Workers repairing products in a bustling workshop.

The shift to circularity is not just about conserving resources but about building a world where industries thrive sustainably, the environment flourishes, and communities find renewed purposes. It is a chance to rewrite the narrative of prosperity one cycle at a time.

Recap and Summary:

1. Key Circular Economy Models:

a. **Product-as-a-Service (PaaS):** Focus on access over ownership, e.g., Philips Lighting as a service.
b. **Sharing economy:** Maximises resource utilisation, e.g., Airbnb and Uber.
c. **Remanufacturing:** Rebuilding products to extend their lifecycle, e.g., Caterpillar's machinery parts.

2. Impacts on Industries and Society:

a. **Economic Resilience:** Reduced dependency on new resources, cost savings, e.g., Patagonia's "Worn Wear."
b. **Environmental Healing:** Reduced waste, GHG emissions, and biodiversity loss, e.g., Kalundborg Eco-Industrial Park.
c. **Social Upliftment:** Creates jobs and strengthens communities, e.g., India's informal recycling sector.

3. Core Idea: Circular economy redefines ownership and transforms waste into opportunities, benefiting the economy, environment, and society while fostering sustainable progress.

FROM WASTE TO WEALTH – THE POWER OF RESOURCE TRANSFORMATION

"Waste is only waste if we waste it."

— William

What is the meaning of Waste to Wealth? Waste becomes a wealth. How is it possible? Well, waste is not just like that: it is discarded without complete use in a linear economy. Now, with innovative ideas, waste can be used in various ways to make different products.

A remarkable transformation is being undergone for the idea of waste. What was once thrown as useless is now seen as a valuable resource filled with opportunities. **By redefining waste, communities and businesses create new economic possibilities, reduce environmental harm, and contribute to a circular economy.** In this chapter, we explore the unbelievable potential of resource recovery, where strategies like recycling, upcycling, and material repurposing turn waste into wealth. From transforming old textiles into fashion to repurposing e-waste and agricultural scraps, this chapter reveals how resource transformation can drive sustainability and unlock a future of shared prosperity.

Power of Resource Recovery

Nature works on the principle that nothing is wasted; the decaying leaves of one season become the fertile soil for the next. Similarly, **the circular economy envisions waste not as the end of a product's life but as the beginning of its transformation into something valuable.** After revealing this, **it is understandable that the power of resource recovery is nothing else but an untapped goldmine or a rich source of wealth desirable for sustainable innovation.**

This waste is not a problem but a possibility. This paradigm shift allows communities and businesses to turn landfills into factories, refuse into restaurants, and scraps into savings.

1. Redefining Waste

In a linear economy, waste is the final step, and it is thrown away. However, **after redefining waste, it can be reused until it reaches its potential. Resource recovery changes this narrative; waste is the final step by turning waste into raw material for new products.**

Let us take the example of Sweden, which converts 99% of its waste into new materials or energy. After minimising landfill use, the city became a waste-to-energy plant power city.

In this scenario, it is crucial to understand how sugarcane can be utilised without generating waste. Each component of the plant is put to use, leaving no residual waste. Let us now examine the functions of this process.

Case Study: Circular Economy in Sugarcane Production

Sugarcane is a prime example of circular economic practice. Initially, cane is processed to extract sugar, and by-products, such as bagasse (fibrous residue), are used to generate bioenergy and make paper. Molasses, another byproduct, is used for ethanol production. The waste left after these processes, such as press mud, serves as a natural fertiliser. Even the final remnants, such as ash from bioenergy plants, are repurposed in road construction, entirely reducing waste. This holistic approach maximises resource efficiency, minimises environmental impacts, and demonstrates a sustainable model for the agricultural industry.

2. Emotional Connection: The Landfill Problem

Resource recovery helps use waste until it reaches its potential and mitigates landfill problems. In this system, waste is no longer waste but becomes a resource.

Imagine a mountain of waste towering over a community—its stench and toxins impacting lives. Now, consider the cyclical economy, which helps you reuse this waste in an innovative way. Imagine those heaps converted into raw materials or clean energy, the fuelling industry, and reducing environmental harm. Eliminating waste is not only one aim of resource recovery; restoring hope is another aim.

3. Case Studies: From Trash to Treasure

Case Study: Coffee Grounds to Ink – Turning Waste into Sustainable Innovation

The issue of disposing of coffee waste is substantial, with numerous used grounds being sent to landfills each day. A startup recognising the untapped potential of this waste began conducting experiments to convert coffee grounds into environmentally friendly printing ink. Their initial efforts focused on creating prototypes using oils and pigments extracted from discarded ground.

Through rigorous testing and collaboration with experts, they refined their products to ensure their quality and compatibility with printers. Monitoring systems track ink performance, market acceptance, and environmental impact.

These results are revolutionary. This new ink provides an eco-friendly option compared to traditional inks, minimising waste and environmental impacts while satisfying consumer preferences for more environmentally responsible products. The project repurposed waste materials and showed how creative solutions can enhance sustainability in common household items.

Case Study: Singapore's NEWater – Transforming Wastewater into a Reliable Resource

Singapore faces the pressing challenge of limited natural water resources to meet the needs of its growing population. Initially, the country relied heavily on imports and rainwater, making water security a key concern. To address this issue, Singapore has begun to explore wastewater recycling.

The NEWater initiative was launched using advanced treatment processes, such as microfiltration, reverse osmosis, and ultraviolet disinfection, to reclaim and convert wastewater into clean and safe drinking water. Pilot projects have tested the technology, and extensive public education campaigns have built trust in the system. Monitoring systems must ensure stringent quality checks to meet international drinking water standards.

The results were transformative. NEWater now supplies a significant portion of Singapore's water demand, reducing reliance on imports and enhancing resilience. This innovative approach secures water resources and sets a global benchmark for sustainable resource recovery.

4. Interactive Prompt

These case studies inspire us about resource recovery by redefining waste.

Now, it is time for you to identify something you consider waste—could it be repurposed? For instance, leftover food scraps could feed a garden or produce biogas.

Make a list of waste things, which you want to redefine.

____

____

____

____

____

Sketch:

A two-part image:

- **Left Side**: A pile of waste in a landfill with emissions rising, symbolising the problem.
- **Right Side**: The same waste transformed into energy, materials, or products like eco-bricks, showcasing a circular solution.

Resource recovery is not just about cleaning up waste but also about discovering new opportunities. By analysing the potential of what we discard, we can reduce environmental burdens, create value, and build a thriving circular economy that turns waste into wealth.

Strategies for Resource Transformation

What is the meaning of resource transformation here? Well, things which is not usable for the purpose that was made, are now it is waste for a particular purpose, but after doing some changes or you may say that after transforming it, you may use it for another purpose. That is called *resource transformation*.

Creativity, purpose, and innovation can transform waste into value. It is like turning a broken vase into a mosaic masterpiece. **By employing strategies such as recycling, upcycling, and material repurposing, we can give new life to discarded resources and redefine waste as wealth.**

1. Recycling: Closing the Loop

The main concept of recycling is recycling a product after use and making it into a new product. In this process, waste becomes raw material for the new product.

Recycling involves processing used materials into new products, conserving raw resources, and reducing environmental impact.

- **Example:** Germany's robust recycling infrastructure achieves a 67% recycling rate, one of the highest globally. This rate turns household waste into materials for new products.
- **Emotional Appeal:** Imagine a plastic bottle you threw away. What if it becomes a cosy fleece jacket or a sturdy park bench instead of polluting the ocean?

2. Upcycling: Adding Value to Waste

After taking something that is no longer in use and giving it a second life and new function in such a way that the finished product becomes more practical, valuable, and beautiful than it previously was, is called upcycling.

Upcycling transforms waste into items of higher quality or artistic value. It focuses on creativity and craftsmanship.

- **Case Study:** TerraCycle's partnership with major brands turns non-recyclable waste, like chip bags, into bags, wallets, and accessories.
- **Interactive Prompt:** This prompt challenges you to identify an item at home that they could upcycle—for example, turning an old ladder into a bookshelf or jars into planters.

Make a list of waste things, which you want to do upcycling with adding value to waste

____

____

____

____

____

____

3. Material Repurposing: Innovative Use of Resources

Reusing waste material for a different purpose but in its original state is called material repurposing. It is really an innovative use of resources.

Material repurposing gives discarded items new functions without significant processing. For example, an old metal can, or bucket can be used as a creative plant container.

- **Example:** In Kenya, Gjenge Makers transforms plastic waste into durable, affordable paving bricks, reducing pollution while creating sustainable infrastructure.

Sketch:

A three-panel illustration:

1. **Recycling:** A used bottle being processed into new products like clothing or benches.
2. **Upcycling:** An artist crafting a decorative lamp from scrap metal
3. **Material Repurposing:** Plastic waste being moulded into colourful paving bricks.

Practical Scenario

Imagine a city waste centre where residents drop off old materials: plastic bottles become park furniture, textiles are transformed into fashion, and construction debris becomes modular housing. These strategies ensure nothing is wasted and everything is valued.

Transforming resources is not just a technical process— it is a mindset shift that challenges us to see potential where others see waste. This is how we pave the way to a sustainable and prosperous future.

Inspiring Case Studies: Transforming Waste into Profitable Resources

Ingenious industries are mastering in turning waste into wealth. That is a seemingly impossible task, similar to spinning straw into gold. **Companies are redefining waste as a resource across textiles, electronics, and agriculture, creating both profit and positive impact.** It is important to understand how to transform waste into profitable resources through inspiring case studies.

1. Textiles: From Waste to Wearable Wonders

The textile industry generates huge waste, but innovators are weaving new opportunities. Let us understand this with a case study:

Case Study: Econyl – Turning Waste into Sustainable Nylon

Plastic waste, particularly discarded fabric scraps and fishing nets, poses a significant environmental threat, especially in marine ecosystems. Recognising this issue, Econyl has begun developing a process to recycle these materials into high-quality nylon.

The journey began with collecting waste materials from landfills, oceans, and factories. Using an innovative regeneration process, the waste was broken down into raw components, reprocessed into nylon fibres. Rigorous quality control and sustainability metrics were implemented to monitor resource savings and environmental impact.

The result was versatile, eco-friendly nylon in luxury fashion and sportswear brands. This initiative prevented tonnes of plastic waste from polluting the environment and conserved resources, setting a standard for circular fashion solutions.

- **Emotional Appeal**: Imagine a bag once tangled in the sea now gracing runways, symbolising redemption and sustainability.

2. Electronics: Mining Urban Gold

Electronic waste, or e-waste, is nothing else but contains valuable metals like gold, silver, and copper. To understand this, let us take an example of **Dell Technologies:**

Dell Technologies - Addressing Electronic Waste Through Circular Practices

This real-world scenario examines Dell Technologies' approach to managing electronic waste.

The rapid rise of e-waste presents a growing environmental challenge, with valuable materials often entering landfills. Dell Technologies has recognised the opportunity to address this issue by introducing a closed-loop recycling programme.

They started by collecting e-waste from customers through take-back programmes and partnerships. Using advanced recycling techniques, Dell extracted valuable materials like plastics, gold, and aluminium to manufacture new devices. To ensure effectiveness, they established monitoring systems to track the material recovery rates and environmental benefits.

This initiative has yielded impressive results. Dell reduced its reliance on raw materials from mining, minimised e-waste, and created a sustainable model for electronic production. This approach addresses the e-waste crisis and aligns with consumer expectations for environmentally responsible technology.

Interactive Prompt: Now, it is your time to consider the fate of your old phones and laptops. Could they be repurposed into something valuable instead of discarded?

3. Agriculture: Turning Trash into Treasure

Agriculture is finding innovative ways to manage organic waste. With the help of a case study, try to learn more about it:

Case Study: AgriProtein – Turning Sustainable Animal Feed from Food Waste

South Africa has faced a dual challenge: managing large amounts of food waste and reducing the environmental impact of traditional animal feed production. AgriProtein saw the opportunity to farm black soldier flies to address both issues.

The company began collecting food waste from restaurants and markets. They used the waste to breed black soldier flies, the larvae of which are rich in protein. The larvae were then processed into high-quality animal feeds. AgriProtein tracked waste diversion rates, feed quality, and environmental impact to monitor success.

The results were transformative. AgriProtein offers a sustainable alternative to traditional feed sources, such as fishmeal, reducing the pressure on natural resources. Their model not only addressed food waste but also demonstrated how nature-inspired innovation can create circular solutions for global challenges.

- **Practical Scenario**: Imagine food scraps from a local market fuelling a new industry that feeds animals, nourishes soil, and reduces landfill burdens.

Sketch:

A three-panel sketch:

1. **Textiles**: Fishing nets are processed into the fabric and displayed as a stylish outfit.
2. **Electronics**: E-waste being dismantled, revealing gold components, and repurposed into a laptop.
3. **Agriculture**: Food waste feeding fly larvae, which are processed into animal feed, closing the loop in farming.

These case studies show that waste is not the end but a new beginning. **By transforming what is discarded, industries are forging a path to prosperity, proving that waste holds untapped potential for innovation, profit, and sustainability.**

Recap and Summary:

1. Power of Resource Recovery:

a. Waste is redefined as a valuable resource, much like nature's cycle, where nothing is wasted.
b. Examples include Circular Economy in Sugarcane Production, Sweden's waste-to-energy plants, and Singapore's NEWater initiative.

2. Strategies for Resource Transformation:

a. **Recycling**: Converts waste into new products, e.g., Germany's 67% recycling rate.
b. **Upcycling**: Adds value to waste, e.g., TerraCycle's creative products.
c. **Material Repurposing**: Reuses waste for different purposes, e.g., Gjenge Makers' plastic paving bricks.

3. Inspiring Case Studies:

a. **Textiles**: Econyl transforms fishing nets into high-quality nylon for fashion.

b. **Electronics**: Dell recycles e-waste for new devices.

c. **Agriculture**: AgriProtein converts food waste into sustainable animal feed.

4. Core Message:

a. Transforming waste into wealth fosters innovation, reduces environmental harm, creates economic value, and builds a sustainable future.

4

CIRCULAR DESIGN AND INNOVATION

"Innovation is the ability to see change as an opportunity — not a threat."

— Steve Jobs

Innovation is as important for a circular economy as breathing is for life. Actually, innovation is the heartbeat of the circular economy.

Innovation is the key to the circular economy. Here, we reimagine the way we design, produce, and consume with creativity and sustainability. In a world facing environmental crises and resource depletion, the circular design is a ray of hope—a game-changer approach, which creates opportunities from challenges. **This chapter explores circular design principles, unveiling how durability, modularity, recyclability, and closed-loop systems can transform industries** with the help of innovative practices and inspiring examples. We will try to understand with the help of the *principle of circular design, examples of circular product and driving innovation in circular economy* how businesses and designers are unfolding solutions that not only reduce waste but also redefine value, and justify that prosperity and sustainability can succeed together.

Principles of Circular Design: Building for a Sustainable Future

Circular Design works on the principle of building a sustainable future. It is like creating a masterpiece meant to stand the test of time, adaptability, and purpose. **Rooted in principles such as durability, modularity, recyclability, and closed-loop systems, it ensures products are not just consumed but continuously renewed. These principles reshape product life cycles, creating systems that minimise waste and maximise value.** Now, let us try to understand all the principles of circular design one by one.

1. Durability: The Pillar of Longevity

Durability is nothing else but a pillar of longevity. **The ability of the physical product to remain working without repair or requiring excessive maintenance is called durability.** Goods with a long usable life are referred to as durable goods.

Durable products reduce the frequency of replacements, so they not only save resources but also minimise waste. Let us take a case study of Patagonia:

Case Study: Patagonia – Durable Gear and Repair Services for Sustainability

Patagonia noticed a common problem in the outdoor gear industry: many products have short lifespans, leading to unnecessary waste and resource depletion. To address this, they committed to creating outdoor gear designed to last for decades, using durable and high-quality materials.

To augment this, Patagonia introduced repair services that allow customers to not discard damaged items but fix them. They also shared tips on maintaining their products to extend their usability. Customer feedback and monitoring the repair programme helped Patagonia enhance its products and services.

This initiative reduces waste, saves resources, and deepens customer trust. By aligning their practices with sustainability values, Patagonia became a leader in responsible outdoor gear, inspiring consumers and competitors.

Interactive Prompt: Now, it is time to reflect on a cherished item you have owned for years. Its durability saved you money as well as reduced environmental impact.

2. Modularity: Designed for Flexibility

Modularity means designed in a flexible way. **It is the quality of consisting of separate parts that, when combined, form a complete whole.** A system lacks modularity when a tweak to one of its components affects the functioning of others.

Modular products can be disassembled, repaired according to need, or upgraded easily. So, there is no need to discard the whole thing; instead, repair or replace the particular part according to need. This saves resources and minimises waste.

Example: Fairphone – Pioneering Sustainable Smartphone Design Through Modularity

Fairphones present an innovative approach to address smartphone production's environmental and social challenges. This company has developed a modular smartphone that allows users to repair and upgrade individual components easily, extending the device's lifespan and reducing electronic waste. Fairphones aim to create a more sustainable and socially responsible supply chain for mobile devices by focusing on the ethical sourcing of materials and improving the working conditions in manufacturing facilities.

- **Practical Scenario**: Consider modular furniture where every piece can be replaced or reconfigured as needs change. That is economical and sustainable.

3. Recyclability: Materials for the Next Cycle

Materials for the next cycle are given by recyclability, without using new resources but from waste. This not only minimises waste but also increases productivity without resource depletion.

Product recyclability means that it can be collected, separated, or otherwise recovered from the waste stream for reuse or use in manufacturing or assembling another item. Products designed for recyclability ensure components can be broken down and reused. Understand this with the help of IKEA's case study.

Case Study: IKEA – Designing for Recyclability and Sustainability

IKEA has recognised the growing environmental concerns surrounding furniture waste and resource-intensive production. Initially, they focused on creating affordable, functional furniture, but they saw an opportunity to integrate sustainability into their design.

They began to use recycled wood and other sustainable materials in their products. At the same time, they reimagined furniture design to ensure items could be easily dismantled, making recycling and reuse simpler for consumers. IKEA has also launched initiatives to collect and recycle furniture. Progress was monitored using material usage reports, customer feedback, and waste reduction metrics.

The outcome is transformative. IKEA reduces the environmental impact and encourages customers to adopt more sustainable habits. Their approach sets a new standard for how large-scale businesses can embed recyclability into their operations, blending affordability with sustainability.

Emotional Appeal: Imagine the satisfaction and happiness after knowing that your discarded table could become part of someone's new bookshelf. After knowing that the part of your beloved things become part of someone's new thing, list down two feelings that you have:

____

____

____

____

____

____

4. Closed-Loop Systems: Waste as a Resource

In closed-loop systems, waste is not generated because it becomes a resource; everything is reused, repaired, shared, or recycled.

In closed-loop systems, every output becomes an input for another process. In this way, it does not generate waste or use new resources.

Case Study: Interface – Innovating Zero Waste with Closed-Loop Systems

Interface, a leading carpet tile manufacturer, recognised a significant issue: the carpet industry generated substantial waste from discarded tiles. To tackle this, Interface committed to developing a closed-loop system where old tiles could be recycled into new ones.

They began by collecting used tiles from customers and investing in advanced recycling technologies to extract and repurpose materials like nylon and backing. Over time, they optimised the process to ensure that the recycled materials met the same quality standards as virgin resources. The progress was tracked through waste diversion rates, material recovery efficiency, and environmental impact assessments.

These results are outstanding. The Interface significantly reduces waste and raw material usage while creating a sustainable production cycle. Their closed-loop system became a model for circular economy practices, demonstrating how industries can achieve profitability while prioritising environmental responsibility.

- **Metaphor:** Nature is the best teacher and resembles the cycle of nature—nourishing the soil to grow new plants After the decomposition of leaves.

Sketch:

A four-part illustration:

1. **Durability:** A rugged backpack lasting through years of use.
2. **Modularity:** A phone with replaceable parts on display.

3. **Recyclability**: Products breaking down into raw materials.
4. **Closed-Loop**: A factory diagram showing waste turned into raw materials.

Circular design is the blueprint for a buoyant future—where products are meant to evolve, endure and inspire, just like stories.

Examples of Circular Products: Designing for a Better Tomorrow

Circular products are the idols of a sustainable economy. They show that responsibility and innovation can coexist. These products consider the essence of circular design— durability, repairability, recyclability, and minimal waste. They are not just products we use; they are stimulators for change. It is important to know about circular products that are designed for a better tomorrow. These are some examples of circular products.

1. Recyclable Packaging: Turning Waste into Opportunity

Recyclable packaging includes any form of packaging that can be reused. Eco-friendly packaging materials include carton board, kraft paper, glassine paper, recycled paper and card, shredded paper, starch adhesive, corrugated cardboardg, and recycled paper.

This finding is significant. In today's world, online marketing is experiencing a surge in popularity, which benefits everyone. However, as Newton's third law states, "for every action, there is an equal and opposite reaction," and this principle also applies to the current situation. While online shopping offers convenience, it also increases waste due to excessive packaging materials. Therefore, addressing this issue when discussing a circular economy is crucial.

Case Study: Loop – A New Way to Think About Packaging

Loop teamed up with brands like Nestlé and Coca-Cola to rethink packaging. Instead of relying on single-use plastics, they introduced sturdy and reusable containers for everyday items.

After customers used the products, they simply returned empty containers to the Loop. The containers were then cleaned, refilled, and returned for reuse. This process was carefully tracked to ensure efficiency and to reduce waste.

Loop helps consumers and companies work together to cut waste and achieve sustainability by making reusable packaging easy and convenient.

Interactive Prompt: Think about the last plastic bottle you tossed—now imagine that as a fresh product, it is returning to the shelf rather than clogging the landfill.

2. Repairable Electronics: Extending Lifespans

Repairable Electronics not only extend lifespans but also minimise e-waste. Therefore, electronics must be repairable.

Case Study: *Fairphones are smartphones that are built with modular components. It is built so that users replace damaged parts, such as batteries or screens, instead of discarding the entire device. This extends its life and reduces electronic waste.*

Metaphor: It is like giving your old car a tune-up rather than trading it in—a practical choice that saves resources and money.

3. Apparel from Recycled Materials: Closing the Textile Loop

Apparel made from recycled materials is very appreciable because it closes the textile loop. This recycled polyester produces nylon from pre-, post-industrial, pre-, or post-consumer waste materials, such as apparel or nylon fishing nets and PET plastic bottles. This promotes a circular economy and diverts materials from landfills.

Case Study: Adidas Ultraboost – Turning Ocean Plastics into Performance Sneakers

Adidas took a bold step towards sustainability by using recycled ocean plastics to create their Ultraboost sneakers. Partnering with the environmental group Parley for the Oceans, they collected plastic waste from coastal areas, preventing it from polluting the seas.

The plastic was then processed into high-performance yarn, which became the foundation for the sneaker's upper material. Adidas monitored the initiative by tracking plastic recovery rates and product performance.

The result was a stylish, durable sneaker that reduced ocean pollution and raised awareness about the potential of turning waste into valuable products.

In the same way, recycled polyester and nylon are used in Patagonia's clothing, the line and proving styles do not have to compromise sustainability.

Emotional Appeal: Imagine wearing a jacket that keeps you warm and helps clean the ocean. Your feelings are at the top of the world.

4. Furniture with a Circular Twist

If a unit is made in such a way that after using a particular piece of furniture to recycle its materials, it can be reused in different ways. These materials were designed as renewable or recycled materials. Resource conservation and sustainable supply chains are prioritised with this circular practices.

Case Study: IKEA's "buy-back" programme is helpful. It allows customers to return old furniture after refurbishment, which is then resold.

Practical Scenario: Imagine your worn-out table finding a second life in someone else's home, creating a reuse chain.

A three-part illustration:

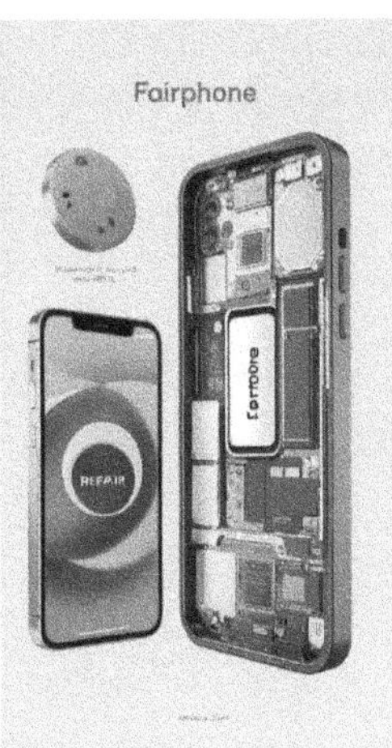

1. **Reusable**: A reusable bottle being cleaned and refilled.
2. **Repairable Electronics**: A Fairphone with its parts being replaced.
3. **Recycled Apparel**: Sneakers with a tag reading "Made from Ocean Plastic."

Circular products are not just items—they are statements of hope, reminding us that every choice we make can weave a better future.

Driving Innovation in Circular Economy: A Creative Revolution

A circular economy is nothing but a creative revolution that is possible only with the help of innovation. Therefore, in a circular economy, innovation involves reimagining a blank canvas, in which every stroke preserves resources, creates value, and takes care of the planet. Designers and businesses rewrite rules by inserting sustainability into the DNA of services and products. It is not just about minimising harm but also about maximising potential. Now let us understand the creative revolution.

1. Designing for Circularity: The Art of Reinvention

Designing for circularity is a design philosophy that aims to promote the recycling and reuse of products and materials and reduce waste.

Designers innovate by creating durable, modular, and repairable products, which guarantee long lifespans and facilitate recycling. In this context, it is important to take case study of Apple:

Case Study: Apple – Redesigning the MacBook for Sustainability

Apple took a significant step toward sustainability by redesigning its MacBook to make it easier to disassemble and recycle. The new design allows for the device's life extension, simpler battery replacements, and reduced electronic waste.

Apple incorporates modular components and fewer adhesives, making recycling more efficient. The company closely monitored the redesign's material recovery rates and environmental impact.

This innovation set a new benchmark for sustainable electronics, demonstrating how thoughtful design can balance performance, durability, and environmental responsibility while inspiring the tech industry to adopt greener practices.

Metaphor: Imagine building a puzzle wherein every piece fits seamlessly and is designed to be reused endlessly.

2. Material Innovation: Beyond the Ordinary

Here, **Material innovation means the application and development of new materials or processes that enable products and resources to circulate within the economy for longer periods while minimising environmental impacts and waste.** It is crucial for the circular economy.

Sustainable materials, such as recycled metals or biodegradable plastics, are transforming industries.

Case Study: Carlsberg – Revolutionising Packaging with the Green Fibre Bottle

Carlsberg took a pioneering step in sustainable packaging by introducing the Green Fibre Bottle, crafted from renewable wood fibres. Designed to replace traditional plastic and glass bottles, this innovative packaging is not only lightweight but also biodegradable.

The journey began with extensive research and collaboration with eco-material experts. Carlsberg rigorously tested the bottle's durability and ability to preserve the quality of beverages.

This initiative aims to significantly reduce environmental impact, offering a sustainable alternative to conventional packaging. By leading the charge in eco-friendly innovation, Carlsberg is setting a new standard for the beverage industry.

Interactive Prompt: If you could invent a sustainable material, how would it benefit the planet and what would it replace? Think about and make a list:

____

____

____

____

____

____

3. Business Model Evolution: Rethinking Value

Here **business model evolution means businesses are moving from selling products to providing services, fostering long-term relationships.** So, businesses or brands can take control of their product's maintenance, repair, reuse, and finally recycling.

Case Study: Rolls-Royce – "Power by the Hour" for Efficiency and Reliability

Rolls-Royce revolutionised the aviation industry with its "Power by the Hour" programme, shifting from selling jet engines to leasing them. Airlines pay based on engine usage, and Rolls-Royce takes full responsibility for maintenance and repairs.

This approach ensures engines run efficiently while reducing downtime and resource waste. By maintaining ownership, Rolls-Royce maximises engine lifespan and recycles components where possible.

The programme promotes resource efficiency, enhances airline reliability, and builds a sustainable business model. It's a win-win innovation demonstrating how service-based strategies can drive sustainability and customer trust.

4. Collaboration as a Catalyst

Collaboration works as a catalyst in circular practices. Partnerships among industries, governments, and innovators drive breakthroughs.

Case Study: Ellen MacArthur Foundation – Driving Circular Practices with Global Brands

The Ellen MacArthur Foundation has been a trailblazer in promoting the circular economy by partnering with global brands like Unilever and H&M. Their collaboration focuses on redesigning business models to eliminate waste, keep materials in use, and regenerate natural systems.

From creating sustainable packaging solutions to developing clothing made from recycled materials, the foundation works closely with its partners to implement innovative, circular practices. Progress is tracked through measurable goals like waste reduction and material reuse.

This initiative inspires industries to rethink traditional models, proving that sustainability and profitability can go hand in hand.

Emotional Appeal: Collaboration reminds us that solving global problems is a symphony of joint efforts and is not a solo act.

Sketch:

A four-panel illustration:

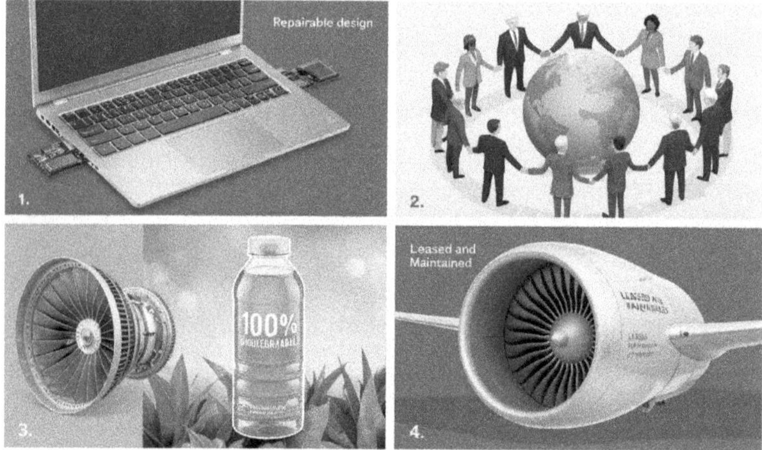

1. **Designing for Circularity**: A laptop with modular, repairable components.
2. **Collaboration**: A globe surrounded by diverse industries, innovators, and governments holding hands.
3. **Material Innovation**: A bottle labelled "100% biodegradable."

4. **Business Model Evolution**: A jet engine with "Leased and Maintained" written underneath.

Circular innovation is the spark lighting the path toward a world where sustainability is more than an aspiration—it is a shared achievement.

Recap and Summary:

Innovation as the Foundation: Circular design relies on innovative thinking to reimagine production and consumption, promoting sustainability and resource efficiency.

1. Principles of Circular Design:

a. **Durability**: Products designed to last longer, reducing waste (e.g., Patagonia's long-lasting gear).
b. **Modularity**: Flexible designs enabling easy repairs and upgrades (e.g., Fairphone's replaceable parts).
c. **Recyclability**: Materials reused to minimise resource depletion (e.g., IKEA's recyclable furniture).
d. **Closed-Loop Systems**: Processes where waste is repurposed as input (e.g., Interface's zero waste carpets).

2. Examples of Circular Products:

a. Recyclable packaging (e.g., Loop's reusable containers).
b. Repairable electronics (e.g., Fairphone).
c. Apparel from recycled materials (e.g., Adidas and Patagonia's recycled lines).

3. Driving Innovation:

a. **Material innovation:** Sustainable materials like Carlsberg's Green Fibre Bottle.
b. **Business model evolution:** Service-based models, e.g., Rolls-Royce's "Power by the Hour."
c. **Collaboration:** Partnerships foster breakthroughs (e.g., Ellen MacArthur Foundation).

This chapter demonstrates that circular design fosters sustainability, minimises waste, and aligns environmental responsibility with economic growth.

5

CIRCULAR BUSINESS MODELS FOR SUSTAINABLE SUCCESS

"The circular economy is not just a trend; it's a blueprint for a resilient, regenerative future where business success and sustainability go hand in hand."

— Ellen MacArthur

In the age of inadequacy of resources and environmental concern, circular business models offer an evolutionary way to success. These models redefine growth by prioritising resilience, sustainability, and long-term value, that is completely different from traditional linear approaches. In this, there is a shift from ownership to access. This shifting optimizes the use of material and adopting reverse logistics, businesses can unlock space for profitability and innovation. Think about a world where every product is part of a regenerative cycle, and waste becomes a wealth. **This chapter looks into the benefits, strategies, and real-world examples of circular models** that show how businesses can flourish while promoting a sustainable future that benefits people and the planet alike.

Defining Circular Business Models: Transforming Commerce for Sustainability

Circular business models (CBMs) drive sustainable transformation. Unlike traditional models focusing on ownership and disposal, these strategies embed responsibility, resilience, and resourcefulness in every stage. Imagine a river flowing continuously, feeding life without losing its essence. This is the essence of business circularity. These are examples of business models.

1. Product-as-a-Service: Shifting from Ownership to Access

PaaS differs from earlier models in that it depends on ownership. However, **in this customer accesses services without owning the products. Companies retain responsibility for maintenance and end-of-life management.**

Example: Philips' "Lighting as a Service" offers lighting solutions where businesses pay for the light, not the fixtures, ensuring better maintenance and recycling.

Case Study: Philips' "Lighting as a Service" — From Product to Service for a Sustainable Future

Traditionally, Philips operated on a linear business model—manufacturing and selling light fixtures outright to customers. The focus was on selling products rather than providing long-term solutions. This approach resulted in customers replacing and discarding old fixtures, contributing to waste and resource depletion.

Recognizing the potential for a more sustainable approach, Philips explored the concept of offering light as a service rather than a product. The idea was simple, yet revolutionary businesses would pay for the light they use, while Philips retained ownership of the fixtures, ensuring they were maintained and recycled responsibly.

Philips began collaborating with large commercial clients to pilot this new model. One notable example is their partnership with Schiphol Airport in Amsterdam. Instead of selling lighting fixtures, Philips installed energy-efficient LED systems while retaining ownership. They handled maintenance and upgrades and ensured the end-of-life recycling of components. The airport paid a service fee based on the quality and intensity of the lighting provided.

Philips closely monitored energy consumption, maintenance needs, and customer feedback. The company used smart sensors to optimize lighting, reducing energy use while maintaining illumination standards. Real-time data allowed Philips to refine their service, ensuring efficiency and customer satisfaction.

This service-based model significantly reduced material waste, extended product lifecycles, and decreased energy consumption for clients. Philips lowered its environmental impact and established long-term client relationships, generating steady revenue. Today, "Lighting as a Service" is a successful example of how circular economy principles can transform industries, benefiting businesses and the environment.

Practical Scenario: Imagine a family that leases high-quality appliances with guaranteed upgrades. There would be no clutter, no e-waste, just convenience. How good it would be.

Interactive Prompt: Would you lease a car or washing machine for convenience and sustainability? Why or why not? List down two reasons:

____

____

____

____

____

____

2. Reverse Logistics: Closing the Loop

Reverse logistics is a state in the supply chain in which the product is returned from the point of sale to the manufacturer or distributor for repair, recovery, disposal, or recycling. It is an efficient system to retrieve, refurbish, or recycle used products, reducing waste and conserving materials.

Case Study: IKEA's "Buy-Back" programme allows customers to return old furniture, which IKEA refurbishes for resale, extending product lifespans. It is a good example of **Reverse Logistics.**

Case Study: IKEA's "Buy-Back" Program — Extending Product Lifecycles through Reverse Logistics

Initially, IKEA followed a linear business model, selling affordable, self-assembled furniture to customers worldwide. While this approach made stylish furniture accessible, it also led to significant waste when customers discarded old or unwanted items. As environmental awareness grew, IKEA faced criticism for contributing to a "throwaway culture."

In response, IKEA explored ways to minimize waste and extend the lifecycle of its products. The company recognized the potential of reverse logistics — a system where products flow back from consumers to the business for recovery, refurbishment, and resale. The "Buy-Back" program was conceived to allow customers to return their used IKEA furniture, reducing waste and maximizing resource efficiency.

The "Buy-Back" program was piloted in selected markets to understand customer response and operational feasibility. Customers could return pre-owned, gently used IKEA furniture in exchange for store credit. Returned items were assessed, refurbished, and resold in the "As-Is" sections of IKEA stores. This ensured that products gained a second life instead of ending up in landfills.

IKEA closely monitored the program's performance through customer feedback, product quality assessments, and environmental impact metrics. Data on the number of products returned, refurbished and resold helped measure success. IKEA also engaged customers through awareness campaigns, promoting the environmental benefits of participating in the "Buy-Back" program.

The initiative successfully extended product lifespans, reduced waste, and strengthened IKEA's sustainability reputation. Customers appreciated the option to recycle their furniture responsibly while receiving store credit. The program has since expanded to multiple countries, contributing to IKEA's goal of becoming a fully circular business by 2030. This case demonstrates how reverse logistics can align profitability with sustainability, creating shared value for businesses, customers, and the environment.

Emotional Appeal: Returning an old item feels less like parting and more like giving it a second life. How rejoiceful feeling is this?

3. Remanufacturing: Turning Old into Gold

Remanufacturing is the building of a product to the specification of the original manufactured product using a combination of reused, repaired, and new parts. It is nothing else but restoring used products to "like new" condition or better, so that they can be used again.

Using parts and materials conserves natural resources, decreases greenhouse gas emissions, and reduces energy consumption. It also helps to prevent toxic substances from being released into the environment.

Case Study: Caterpillar's "Reman" programme remanufactures heavy equipment parts, saving energy and resources while providing affordable alternatives.

Case Study: Caterpillar's "Reman" Program — Pioneering Circularity in Heavy Equipment Manufacturing

Initially, Caterpillar operated a traditional linear manufacturing model, producing and selling heavy equipment parts like engines, hydraulics, and drive trains. Once these components reached the end of their life, they were often discarded, contributing to significant waste and resource depletion. Additionally, the high cost of brand-new parts created a challenge for customers seeking affordable yet reliable alternatives.

Recognizing the need to reduce waste while offering cost-effective solutions, Caterpillar began exploring the remanufacturing concept— restoring end-of-life components to their original performance standards. In the 1970s, the company initiated the "Reman" program, focusing on remanufacturing used parts instead of producing new ones from scratch. This marked a significant shift toward a circular economy approach.

Under the "Reman" program, used components are collected from customers, disassembled, cleaned, and inspected. Worn-out parts are replaced, and functional components are refurbished to meet strict quality standards. The remanufactured parts are then sold at a fraction of the cost of new ones, backed by the same warranty. Caterpillar invested in advanced technologies and skilled labor to ensure high-quality remanufacturing processes.

Caterpillar tracks key performance indicators (KPIs) like material recovery rates, energy savings, and customer satisfaction to monitor the program's success. Feedback loops with customers help refine processes, ensuring that remanufactured parts meet performance expectations. The company also measures environmental impact, such as reduced carbon emissions and raw material consumption.

The "Reman" program has been a resounding success, saving substantial energy and raw materials while reducing landfill waste. It also provides customers with affordable, high-quality parts, strengthening brand loyalty and expanding market reach. By prioritizing circular practices, Caterpillar has solidified its reputation as a leader in sustainable manufacturing, proving that profitability and environmental stewardship can go hand in hand.

Metaphor: It is like taking a worn-out symphony and playing it again with refreshed instruments—beautiful and impactful.

Practical Scenario: A small business owner opts for remanufactured machinery, balancing cost and sustainability.

4. Sharing Economy

A sharing economy is an economic model in which goods and resources are shared by individuals and groups in a collaborative way such that physical assets become services. It enables people and organisations to earn profits from underutilised resources. In this, there is a collaborative consumption where people share access to products or services.

Examples: Platforms like Airbnb and bike-sharing systems optimise resource use by pooling assets.

Case Study: Airbnb — Revolutionizing the Sharing Economy Through Resource Optimization

Before Airbnb's inception, the hospitality industry was predominantly linear, relying on traditional hotels and resorts for accommodation. Vacant homes, extra rooms, and underutilized properties existed worldwide, but there was no organized way to connect these resources with travelers seeking affordable and unique lodging experiences. Additionally, homeowners lacked a platform to monetize their unused spaces effectively.

Airbnb was founded in 2008 by Brian Chesky, Joe Gebbia, and Nathan Blecharczyk. They initially aimed to help people rent out air mattresses in their apartments to conference attendees when hotel rooms were scarce. The idea of utilizing existing spaces rather than constructing new ones quickly gained traction, signaling a shift from a linear to a sharing economy. By leveraging technology, Airbnb created a platform that connected hosts willing to rent out their properties with guests seeking cost-effective, personalized stays.

Airbnb expanded globally, building a user-friendly platform accessible through mobile apps and websites. They implemented a review system to build trust between hosts and guests, introduced secure payment methods, and established clear guidelines for both parties. The platform continually evolved, offering insurance for hosts, verified identification for users, and customer support to enhance the experience. They also used data analytics to understand user preferences, optimize pricing, and enhance listings.

Airbnb monitors its platform through user feedback, reviews, and data analytics, ensuring quality experiences while mitigating illegal rentals or property misuse. They adjust their policies according to local regulations and collaborate with governments to support responsible hosting. Airbnb's success metrics include the number of active listings, booking rates, customer satisfaction, and revenue growth.

Airbnb has transformed the accommodation industry, provided affordable, diverse lodging options while helping homeowners generate income from underutilized spaces. The platform optimizes resource use, reduces the need for new construction, and minimizes environmental impact. Airbnb's success story exemplifies how the sharing economy can create value through resource efficiency, benefiting hosts, guests, and communities.

Case Study: Bike-Sharing Systems — Optimizing Resource Use in the Sharing Economy

Before the emergence of organized bike-sharing systems, urban transportation relied heavily on private vehicles and public transit. Bicycles, although present, were primarily used by individual owners, leading to underutilized assets. Traffic congestion, rising pollution, and limited public transportation options in densely populated cities highlighted the need for sustainable and efficient transport solutions.

The bike-sharing concept began in the 1960s with the "White Bicycle Plan" in Amsterdam, where free-to-use bicycles were provided for public use. However, due to theft and misuse, the initiative failed. Technological advancements in the late 1990s and early 2000s allowed for secure, trackable, and sustainable bike-sharing systems. Cities like Paris, with its successful "Vélib'" program launched in 2007, demonstrated the potential of bike-sharing to optimize urban mobility. These systems used docking stations, digital tracking, and secure payment methods to address initial challenges.

Modern bike-sharing systems use GPS-enabled bikes, mobile applications, and digital payment platforms to provide convenient and accessible services. Users can locate, unlock, and pay for bikes through smartphone apps, reducing the need for private ownership. Cities partner with private operators or establish public-private collaborations to install docking stations, maintain bikes, and ensure smooth operations. Marketing campaigns promote the benefits of eco-friendly, last-mile connectivity, encouraging more users to adopt bike-sharing.

Through data analytics, bike-sharing systems track usage patterns, popular routes, and demand peaks. Regular maintenance schedules and user feedback help maintain the quality and safety of the bicycles. Monitoring mechanisms also prevent theft and vandalism. Cities adjust their strategies by adding more docking stations, integrating with public transit, and providing incentives like discounted rides during off-peak hours.

Today, bike-sharing systems operate in numerous cities worldwide, reducing traffic congestion, lowering carbon emissions, and promoting healthier lifestyles. These platforms exemplify the sharing economy's ability to optimize resource use by maximizing the utility of bicycles as shared assets. The success of bike-sharing has inspired similar sharing economy models, such as e-scooter sharing, demonstrating the potential of pooled assets in achieving sustainable urban mobility.

Emotional Appeal: Sharing fosters community while reducing environmental strain, reminding us of the power of collective action.

Sketch:

Four-panel illustration:

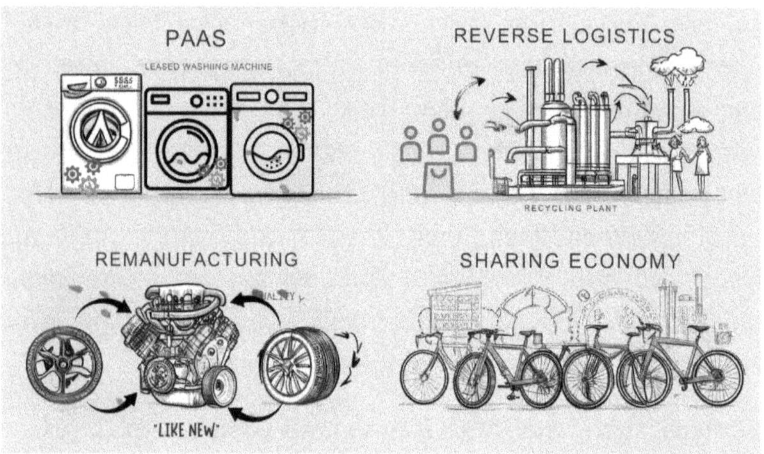

i. **PaaS**: A leased washing machine with a maintenance icon.

ii. **Reverse Logistics**: Arrows pointing from consumers to a recycling plant.

iii. **remanufacturing**: A refurbished engine labelled "Like New."

iv. **sharing economy**: A community hub with shared bikes and tools.

These models represent the ingenuity driving sustainability, transforming wasteful practices into opportunities for lasting success.

Financial and Environmental Benefits: Unlocking Value in Circular Models

Reusing and recycling products can slow the use of natural resources, reduce habitat disruption and landscape erosion,

and help limit biodiversity loss. Another benefit of circular models is the total annual greenhouse gas emissions reduction.

Circular business models offer a situation where everyone experiences positive results or benefits. This is a win-win scenario that merges cost savings with environmental conservation. Suppose it is a golden key that opens the door to profits and safeguards the planet. This is the power of circular practice. Now, it is time to dive deep into financial and environmental benefits through circular models

1. Cost Savings Through Resource Efficiency

Resource efficiency refers to maximising the benefits of products or services, while minimising consumption and waste. **By designing products for reuse, repair, and recycling, companies remarkably cut the costs of raw materials and waste disposal. Thus, with the help of circular practices, there is cost savings through resource efficiency.**

Study on Remanufacturing Profitability: A study by Lund (2018) found that remanufactured products require 50-75% less energy than new production, leading to significant cost savings. Companies such as Caterpillar have reported increased profit margins by adopting remanufacturing.

Case Study: Renault – Saving Resources with Remanufactured Car Parts

Renault has set a benchmark in sustainable manufacturing at its Choisy-le-Roi plant, where it remanufactures car parts like engines, gearboxes, and fuel systems. Refurbishing used components uses 80% less energy than producing new parts.

The initiative began by focusing on reducing costs and environmental impact while delivering high-quality, reliable parts. Regular monitoring ensured that energy savings and waste reduction were maximised.

This approach saves Renault millions annually and demonstrates how circular practices can create a win-win for businesses and the planet by cutting emissions and conserving resources.

Metaphor: It is like squeezing juice from an orange, then using the peel for zest—extracting every bit of the value.

2. Waste Reduction Translates to Savings

Reducing waste will not only protect the environment but also reduce expenses or save on disposal costs. It lowers landfill fees and diminishes environmental cleanup costs. Let's examine how Interface demonstrates the conversion of waste reduction into savings through an example.

Case Study: Interface – Achieving Sustainability with "Mission Zero"

Interface, a global carpet manufacturer, transformed its operations through its ambitious "Mission Zero" initiative, aiming to eliminate negative environmental impacts. The company shifted to using recycled materials in its carpets and focused on waste reduction across its supply chain.

Over a decade, Interface saved $450 million by cutting waste and energy use, proving that sustainability can drive financial success. Continuous monitoring ensured the initiative stayed on track.

"Mission Zero" not only minimised Interface's environmental footprint but also set a powerful example for other industries,

showcasing how green practices can align with profitability and innovation.

> **Ellen MacArthur Foundation Reports**: Circular business models could reduce global waste by up to 45% by 2050. Reverse logistics, a core component, ensures that 80% of used materials can be recycled or reused, mitigating landfill overflow and pollution.

Interactive Prompt: Reflect on your daily routine—how could reusing or sharing an item reduce your expenses?

3. Enhanced Brand Image and Consumer Loyalty

Sustainable practices build trust and attract environmentally conscious consumers. Circular models enhance brand image and consumers' support in this way.

Case Study: Patagonia's "Worn Wear" programme promotes repair and resale of used clothing, boosting sales and fostering customer loyalty.

Emotional Appeal: Supporting circular brands feels like being part of a global movement for good, a reason for consumers to take pride in their choices.

4. Environmental Impact Fuels Financial Gains

The benefit of circular models is the reduction in total annual greenhouse gas emissions. They also reduce habitat disruption and landscape erosion and help limit biodiversity loss. Circular businesses align with ESG (Environmental, Social, Governance) goals, attracting investments and government incentives, fueling financial benefits.

Case Study: IKEA's circular furniture initiatives reduced emissions and positioned the brand as a sustainability leader.

> **Carbon Footprint Analysis**: A life-cycle assessment (LCA) conducted by the European Environment Agency (2021) showed that circular practices reduce greenhouse gas emissions by 56% compared to traditional linear models. For example, recycled aluminium saves 95% of the energy required for primary aluminium production.

Sketch:

A four-panel illustration:

1. **Cost Savings:** A factory producing remanufactured car parts with lower energy usage.
2. **Waste Reduction:** A landfill shrinking as products are diverted for recycling.
3. **Environmental Impact:** A tree growing from coins, symbolising financial and ecological harmony.

4. **Brand Image:** Customers lining up at a store labelled "Eco-Friendly and Trusted."

The four-panel representation of the sustainability concepts: cost savings, waste reduction, environmental impact, and brand image.

Steps to Implement a Circular Business Model: A Roadmap for Success

"The only impossible journey is the one you never begin"

– Tony Robbins

Circular economy roadmaps are a strategic tool for promoting a comprehensive change. They are a concrete and practical solution for achieving success.

Transitioning to a circular business model is like planting a seed—it requires care, patience, and the right conditions. And its rewards are a flourishing, sustainable enterprise. Here is a guide that helps startups and established businesses make the shift step-by-step.

1. Rethink Design Principles

It is important to rethink the principle of design. Thus, start by designing products that are durable, repairable, and recyclable. This will help minimise waste and extend their life span.

Let us take Fairphone as an example. This modular smartphone company designs phones with replaceable parts to minimise waste and extend their lifespan.

Practical Tip: It is important to conduct a product lifecycle assessment to identify areas for improvement.

Metaphor: It is like crafting a house of bricks instead of straw—built to last.

2. Optimise Resource Use

Well, as the title suggests, optimising resource use is important for circular practices. This is only possible through the reuse of resources until their capacity ends.

The transition from a linear supply chain to a closed-loop system is optimised resource use.

Let us take Unilever's "Love Beauty and Planet" line as an example. It uses recycled materials for packaging, reducing its carbon footprint.

Interactive Prompt: Map your supply chain. Which materials can be sourced sustainably or reused?

3. Develop Reverse Logistics

Reverse logistics is a state in the supply chain in which the product is returned from the point of sale to the manufacturer or distributor for recovery, recycling, repair, or disposal. Thus, **it is important to create systems for collecting, refurbishing, and reselling used products.**

Example: Dell's recycling programme recovers precious metals like gold from old electronics, turning waste into value.

Practical Tip: Partner with logistics firms to streamline returns and refurbishment.

4. Foster Consumer Engagement

Yes, **fostering consumer engagement is not only a requirement but also an essential condition for circular practices. Awareness programmes and education play a crucial role in this.** So, educating and incentivising customers to participate in the circular model is very helpful. The Case Study of H&M's garment collection initiative is a good example of this.

Case Study: H&M – Encouraging Recycling Through Garment Collection

H&M introduced a garment collection initiative to tackle textile waste while promoting recycling. Customers can return old or unwanted clothing at H&M stores, regardless of the brand, and receive discounts on future purchases as an incentive.

The collected garments are sorted and either reused, recycled into new fabrics, or repurposed for other industries. H&M closely tracks the volume of collected clothing and its recycling outcomes.

This initiative reduces textile waste and raises awareness about sustainable fashion. It encourages consumers to embrace recycling while aligning with H&M's commitment to a circular economy.

Emotional Appeal: Empowering customers to be part of the change fosters loyalty and pride.

5. Collaborate Across Sectors

As the saying goes, one swallow does not make a summer. **Circular practices are not possible alone. But to achieve this, it is important to work with governments, NGOs, and** other businesses. Collaboration across sectors is necessary to scale circular solutions.

Case Study: CE100 – Collaboration for a Sustainable Future

The Circular Economy 100 (CE100), an initiative by the Ellen MacArthur Foundation, brings together businesses, governments, and researchers to promote circular economy practices. The programme creates a platform for sharing ideas, exchanging expertise, and developing innovative solutions to reduce waste and better use resources.

Through collaborative workshops and challenges, members work on practical ways to implement circular strategies. By uniting diverse organisations, CE100 fosters creativity and drives progress toward sustainable systems. It demonstrates how teamwork and shared knowledge can pave the way for a more resource-efficient and environmentally friendly future.

Policy Support: Research from the OECD emphasises that public-private partnerships accelerate the adoption of circular models, with governments incentivising innovations through tax breaks and grants for circular enterprises.

Sketch:

A five-step circular pathway:

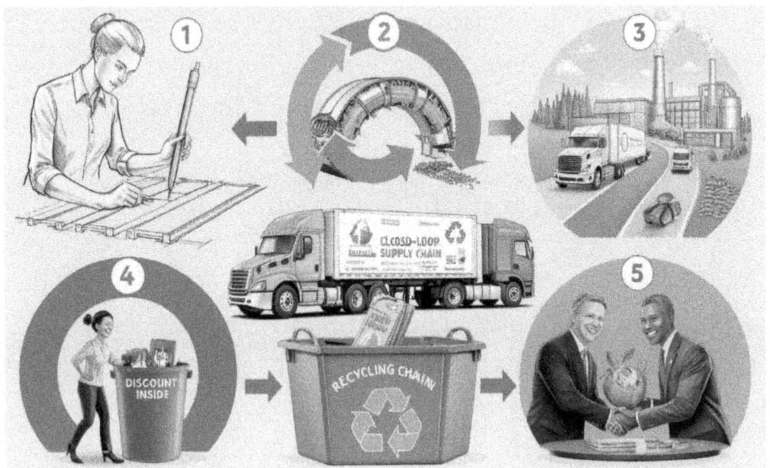

1. **Design**: A designer sketching a durable, modular product.
2. **Resource Use**: A supply chain loop highlighting reused materials.
3. **Reverse Logistics**: Trucks returning used products to factories.
4. **Consumer Engagement**: A customer dropping items into a recycling bin labelled "Discount Inside!"
5. **Collaboration**: Diverse entities (companies, governments) shaking hands over a globe.

By following these steps, businesses can transition from a linear approach to one that drives profits and protects the planet for future generations.

Recap and Summary:

Understanding Circular Models:

Circular business models emphasise maximising resource efficiency, reducing waste, and increasing product lifecycles with approaches like product-as-a-service, reverse logistics, and remanufacturing.

Financial and Environmental Benefits:

These models reduce waste, save costs, magnify brand reputation, and stimulate customer loyalty, driving sustainability and profit.

Steps for Implementation:

Rethink Design: Prioritise recyclability and durability.

Optimise Resources: Closing the loop in supply chains.

Reverse Logistics: It enables product returns for refurbishment.

Consumer Engagement: Create Awareness and Incentivise participation in circular practices.

Collaboration: Collaboration with stakeholders is important to scale solutions.

Inspiring Case Studies:

Examples include Fairphone's modular design, H&M's garment return initiative, and Dell's e-waste recycling, which are inspiring for taking things further.

This chapter underscores how businesses can thrive by adopting sustainable practices and innovations that align with environmental responsibility and economic growth.

Reflective Questions:

- How many items in your daily life could be reused or shared instead of discarded? Make a quick list of five.

\
\
\
\
\
\

- Think of an old item you own. How would you feel if you could refurbish it instead of throwing it away? Write down your feeling in one word:

6

POLICIES AND REGULATIONS – THE ROLE OF GOVERNMENT

"Good governance is perhaps the single most important factor in eradicating poverty and promoting development."

— Kofi Annan

Policies and regulations were important in the transition from linear to circular. Without the guidance of effective regulations and policies, a circular economy cannot flourish. Governments play a crucial role in setting the framework for businesses, communities, and individuals to transition from wasteful linear practices to sustainable circular systems that work as fuel for change by creating incentives, imposing standards, and encouraging innovation. It transforms ambitious visions into actionable realities. In this chapter, we explore how forward-looking regulations, universal success stories, and cooperative public-private initiatives can push the circular transition. **Bold governance can pave the way for a prosperous and sustainable future as the foundations of modern societies are built by laws.**

The Role of Policy in Circular Transition: A Government-Led Revolution

Government policies and incentives are nothing else but the wind beneath the wings or may say that such type of support system that the circular economy does not succeed without it. They **guide businesses, inspire innovation, and enable citizens to adopt sustainable practices.** Without these policies, circular initiatives are like seeds scattered on rocky ground—promising but unlikely to flourish. Without government policies, circular initiatives start with joy, but last for a short time. Now, let us understand how this works.

1. The Foundation of Circular Success: Enabling Policies

Effective policies can help scale up and accelerate circular economic actions. These policies not only support businesses in overcoming obstacles by encouraging innovative projects and long-term investment but also facilitate collaboration and partnerships to produce tangible results. In simple words, **policies ensure fair play and remove barriers to circular transition.**

Case Study: European Union – Leading Circularity with CEAP

The European Union launched the Circular Economy Action Plan (CEAP) as a bold roadmap to reduce waste and make products more sustainable. CEAP focuses on circular product design, encouraging goods that are durable, reusable, and easier to recycle.

With clear goals and policies, the plan addresses key sectors like electronics, textiles, and plastics, pushing for innovation and sustainable practices. The EU monitors progress through measurable targets, fostering accountability.

CEAP has positioned the EU as a global leader in circularity, setting an example of how ambitious planning can drive sustainable growth while preserving the environment for future generations.

> **Scientific Evidence**: A 2021 study in *Nature Sustainability* found that nations with supportive circular policies saw a 15-20% increase in resource efficiency within a decade.

Interactive Prompt: Imagine you are the leader of a country. What was the first policy to reduce waste and boost resource efficiency?

---

2. Incentivising Innovation: Pushing the Circular Agenda

In this context, innovation incentives are the drivers or mechanisms that stimulate and inspire individuals or companies to create novel ideas, products, or processes for circular practices. These incentives promote engagement and provide recognition to businesses and people who implement circular approaches. Thus, **the act of incentivising innovation serves not only to motivate participants but also to improve and expand circular practices.**

Case Study: Japan – Leading the Way in E-Waste Management

Japan introduced the Home Appliance Recycling Law, which ensures that old appliances, such as TVs, air conditioners, and refrigerators, are recycled instead of discarded to combat the rising issue of e-waste. Before this law, valuable resources such as rare Earth metals were often lost, and waste management posed environmental challenges.

This law made manufacturers responsible for collecting and recycling used appliances. Recycling centres were established, and strict monitoring systems ensured compliance and efficiency.

This initiative significantly reduced e-waste, recovered precious materials, and promoted sustainable practices and made

Japan a global example of effective resource management and environmental responsibility.

Practical Scenario: A startup using recycled ocean plastics receives tax breaks, enabling them to scale operations while promoting sustainability.

3. Aligning Citizens and Businesses: Collaborative Frameworks

This study explores the vital importance of regulatory frameworks in fostering and facilitating effective collaboration between corporations and individuals to promote circular economic strategies. These policies establish a unified vision for action and accountability, ensuring the shift from a linear to a circular economic model is meaningful, comprehensive, and sustainable. Essentially, such regulations unite various stakeholders around a shared objective.

Case Study: Singapore – Reducing Food Waste with the Zero Waste Master Plan

Singapore's Zero Waste Master Plan addressed the challenge of tackling rising food waste, which was filling up landfills and wasting valuable resources. Initially, the food waste was discarded without exploring recycling options.

The government introduced grants to support food waste recycling technologies to address this issue and launched public education campaigns to raise awareness. These efforts have encouraged the development of composting, biogas production, and other sustainable practices. The progress was closely monitored through regular waste audits and community feedback.

This initiative successfully reduced landfill-bound food waste by 40%, proving that education and innovation can lead to impactful environmental solutions.

Emotional Appeal: Imagine a community where citizens, industries, and governments work as one— harmony that transforms waste into opportunities.

Sketch:

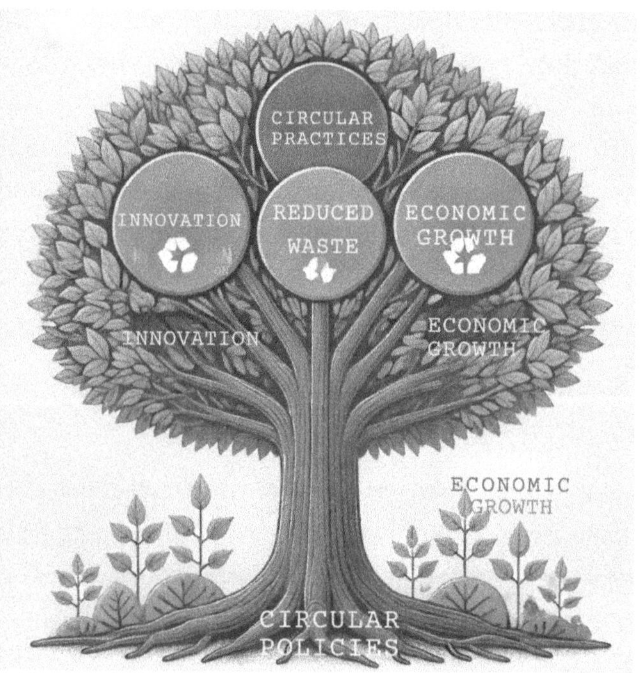

1. Here is a visual representation of the Policy Impact tree diagram, showing "Circular Policies" as the roots and "Innovation," "Reduced Waste," and "Economic Growth" as the branches, symbolising the outcomes of effective circular policies.

2. Illustrating a factory recycling products under a government-funded scheme, showcasing the banner "Tax Credit for Circularity" and emphasising sustainability with green energy elements like wind turbines and solar panels. It highlights the seamless integration of policy support and industrial practices

Government policies are the architects of a circular future, laying pathways that balance economic growth, environmental preservation, and societal well-being. Like a symphony conductor, they ensure every stakeholder plays their part in harmony for a sustainable tomorrow.

Examples of Effective Policies Globally: Circular Economy Success Stories

Research has demonstrated that well-crafted government policies can catalyse the shift from a linear economy to a circular economy. These policies serve as beacons, not only steering countries through the turbulent waters of waste accumulation and resource scarcity but also illuminating the path to economic growth and environmental sustainability. Let us examine successful global policies that illustrate the effectiveness of the circular economy when implemented with appropriate rules and regulations.

1. Europe: The Pioneer of Circular Frameworks

Europe is at the forefront of the implementation of structured policies that encourage innovation and responsibility. The continent has embraced the sharing economy, promoting initiatives such as car sharing, and has significantly improved its recycling efforts. Europeans have reduced the demand for new raw materials across their production and consumption processes. Through these actions, **Europe established itself as a trailblazer in the circular economy movement.**

Case Study: The European Union's *Circular Economy Action Plan (CEAP)*. This comprehensive policy targets areas, such as electronics, plastics, and textiles. It mandates extended producer responsibility (EPR), which requires companies to manage the lifecycle of their products.

> **Scientific Evidence**: Studies indicate that the CEAP could reduce the EU's greenhouse gas emissions by 50% by 2050, underscoring its environmental impact.

Metaphor: Think of Europe as a gardener planting seeds of innovation that bloom into sustainable practices.

2. Asia: Innovative and Culturally Rooted Policies

The rich cultural, economic, environmental, and social diversity within Asia has led each country to develop its interpretation and implementation of circular economic principles. These diverse approaches underscore the localisation of the circular economy being localised in Asia, shaped by traditions and regional cultural values, allowing each country to adopt circular economy principles in its specific context. In fact, **Asia integrates circular principles with rapid industrial growth.**

Case Study: Japan's *Home Appliance Recycling Law* requires manufacturers to recycle refrigerators, air conditioners, and washing machines. Over 80% of components are reused, reducing waste and conserving resources.

Interactive Scenario: Imagine as a Japanese appliance maker—How would you design products to align with recycling mandates and lower costs?

3. Elsewhere: Diverse Approaches, Shared Goals

These are examples of the circular practices adopted by different countries.

Singapore: The *Zero Waste Masterplan* incentivises food waste recycling and promotes public awareness campaigns. Its implementation has reduced food waste by 40% within a decade.

South Africa: Policies encourage tyre recycling, leading to innovative products, such as paving materials and furniture.

Chile: The *Plastics Law* bans single-use plastics in restaurants, drastically reducing plastic pollution.

Emotional and Societal Angle

Such strategies not only minimise waste but also create employment opportunities, encourage inventiveness, and promote a collective sense of accountability. Picture the satisfaction of residing in a country where discarded materials are transformed into valuable resources, and creative solutions are applauded.

Table of Effective Policies Globally: Circular Economy Success Stories

Country	Policy/ Program	Objective	Key Measures	Impact/ Outcome
European Union	**EU Circular Economy Action Plan**	Transition to a circular economy across member states	Eco-design regulations, waste reduction targets, extended producer responsibility (EPR)	Significant waste reduction, increased recycling rates, and innovation in sustainable design
Sweden	**Tax Reduction on Repairs**	Reduce waste by extending product life	Lowered VAT on repair services for electronics and household goods	Boosted repair industry, decreased landfill waste, and promoted a culture of reuse
Netherlands	Circular Amsterdam	Become 100% circular by 2050	Circular construction regulations, resource mapping, collaboration between government and private sectors	Increased circular construction projects, reduced material consumption, and stimulated green innovation
India	**E-Waste Management Rules, 2016**	Tackle growing e-waste and promote recycling	Extended Producer Responsibility (EPR), collection targets for e-waste, incentives for recycling units	Improved formal e-waste recycling, enhanced awareness, and better compliance by electronic manufacturers

Country	Policy/ Program	Objective	Key Measures	Impact/ Outcome
Japan	**Home Appliance Recycling Law**	Promote recycling of electronic waste	Manufacturers required to collect and recycle discarded appliances	Over 70% recycling rate for home appliances, reduced e-waste, and valuable material recovery
China	**Circular Economy Promotion Law**	National-level circular economy model	Mandatory recycling, closed-loop production, circular industrial parks	Enhanced resource efficiency, waste-to-energy projects, and reduced environmental pollution
Finland	**Roadmap to a Circular Economy 2035**	Establish a carbon-neutral, circular economy	Investment in sustainable innovation, public-private partnerships, education for circular skills	Increased circular business models, enhanced R&D in circular technologies, and global leadership in sustainability
France	**Anti-Waste Law for a Circular Economy**	Reduce waste, ban single-use plastics	Ban on disposable plastic products, anti-food waste measures, EPR expansion	Significant reduction in single-use plastic use, decrease in food waste, and increased recycling rates
South Korea	**Resource Circulation Policy**	Minimize waste and increase recycling	Waste charge system, mandatory recycling of specific materials, circular manufacturing incentives	Notable increase in recycling rates, reduction of waste-to-landfill, and higher resource recovery

Country	Policy/Program	Objective	Key Measures	Impact/Outcome
Germany	**Closed Substance Cycle and Waste Management Act**	Minimize landfill waste and increase material recovery	Strict recycling targets, landfill bans, promotion of circular manufacturing	Germany achieves one of the highest recycling rates globally, reducing landfill dependency
Kenya	**Plastic Bag Ban (2017)**	Eliminate plastic pollution and promote sustainable alternatives	Total ban on plastic bags, heavy fines for violations	Significant drop in plastic pollution, cleaner cities, and increased eco-friendly alternatives

The above table provides a perspective on how countries across continents are effectively implementing policies to foster a circular economy.

Sketch:

Following sketch shows several regions around the world have successfully implemented circular economy (CE) practices, serving as global benchmarks for sustainability and resource efficiency. Here are some of the most notable ones:

- **Policy-Driven Success:** The EU and Japan show that strong policies accelerate CE adoption.
- **Industrial Symbiosis:** China and the Nordic countries demonstrate how waste can become a valuable resource.
- **Corporate Leadership:** The U.S. highlights how companies can drive circularity.
- **Grassroots Circularity:** India's decentralised approach to CE offers valuable lessons in localised solutions.

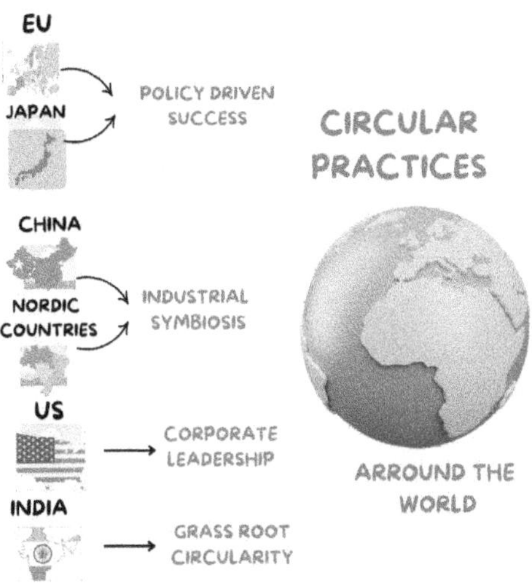

Global Policy Map: Highlight regions with effective circular policies,

These strategies illustrate that, regardless of geographical location or cultural background, the transition to a circular economy is not only feasible but also beneficial showcasing the effectiveness of cooperative efforts and forward-thinking approaches.

Public-Private Partnerships: Bridging Forces for Circular Economy Adoption

Public-private partnerships work as a bridging force for circular economy adoption. They play a vital role in achieving circular practices. A circular economy relies on resource efficiency and sustainable production and consumption. These are the central concepts in achieving sustainable development, which is only possible through PPP.

Imagine a symphony in which each instrument plays a part, creating harmony. Public-private partnerships (PPPs) are symphonies in the circular economy, blending governmental authority with business innovation to create impactful solutions for sustainability.

1. The Role of Governments in PPPs

Governments create an enabling environment through policy frameworks, financial support, and regulatory incentives that encourage private sector involvement. By promoting partnerships, they facilitate the expansion and innovation of circular economic initiatives, including waste conversion projects and eco-friendly industrial zones. This collaborative approach optimises resource utilisation, enhances adoption rates, and promotes sustainable growth in line with societal and environmental objectives.

Governments set this stage by offering incentives, regulations, and infrastructure.

Example: The Dutch government collaborates with companies under the *Netherlands Circular Economy Programme*. By 2050, it aims to achieve a fully circular economy focusing on construction, plastics, and agriculture.

> **Scientific Evidence:** Research from the World Economic Forum highlights that PPPs reduce the financial risks of circular initiatives and foster long-term investments.

2. Businesses: Innovation and Execution

Businesses: innovation and execution play an important role in circular practices. It underscores the crucial functions of businesses in promoting sustainable practices. **By engaging with stakeholders and embedding sustainability into their core functions, organisations convert challenges into prospects, enhancing profitability while simultaneously contributing to environmental conservation and fostering a robust, future-oriented economy.**

Corporations provide agility, resources, and innovative solutions to accelerate their implementation.

Case Study: Coca-Cola – Tackling Plastic Waste with RAIN in Africa

Through its Replenish Africa Initiative (RAIN), Coca-Cola joined hands with governments across Africa to address the growing issue of plastic waste. Recognising the need for sustainable solutions, this initiative focused on building recycling plants and running public awareness campaigns to encourage responsible waste management.

By collaborating with local communities and stakeholders, Coca-Cola ensures that the programme is impactful and inclusive. Progress is regularly evaluated in order to expand its reach and efficiency.

This partnership has significantly improved the recycling infrastructure while fostering awareness about plastic waste, setting an example of how public-private collaboration can drive meaningful environmental change.

Metaphor: Picture river (government policies) carving paths, while tributaries (businesses) provide flow and sustenance, creating a thriving ecosystem.

3. Co-Developed Projects: Success Stories

These are examples of success stories of Co-developed projects in the circular economy, which motivate us to take further action. Inspiration is very important to achieve it.

Case Studies:

India – Managing Plastic Waste with Extended Producer Responsibility (EPR)

India's Extended Producer Responsibility (EPR) framework has brought companies like Nestlé and PepsiCo together with municipalities to address the growing plastic waste problem. Under EPR, these companies take responsibility for managing the waste generated from their products, including their collection, recycling, and disposal.

Collaborating with local governments, they implement efficient waste management systems and raise awareness of recycling among communities. Regular audits ensure accountability and progress.

This initiative not only reduces plastic pollution but also encourages shared responsibility among producers, making it a significant step toward cleaner and more sustainable India.

Finland – Cutting Construction Waste with Collaborative Efforts

Finland has taken an innovative approach to reduce construction waste by fostering public-private partnerships (PPPs). Previously, a large number of reusable materials, such as concrete and steel, were used in landfills, contributing to environmental challenges.

By working together, government agencies and private companies developed systems to salvage and repurpose these materials. This collaboration also encourages innovation and strict waste management practices.

As a result, Finland successfully reduced construction waste by 30%, providing an inspiring example of how teamwork and sustainable practices can create a greener future in the building industry.

USA – Transforming Recycling with the Closed-Loop Fund

The Closed-Loop Fund in the USA, which focuses on improving recycling infrastructure, is a groundbreaking public-private partnership (PPP). Recognising the need for sustainable waste management, this initiative provides financial support to cities and businesses for building efficient recycling systems.

By investing in innovative technologies and modern equipment, funds can help reduce landfill waste and increase the recovery of valuable materials. Regular progress assessments ensure that projects have lasting impacts.

This initiative not only supports long-term waste management but also demonstrates how collaboration between the public and private sectors can drive meaningful environmental progress.

4. Emotional and Societal Benefits

Imagine a child growing up in a city where waste bins turn plastic into playgrounds, a testament to collective action for a better tomorrow. If imagination gives so much amusement, what happens when it becomes reality? Thus, it is now time to work together to successfully achieve our goal for a better future.

Interactive Prompt: If you were part of a PPP, what innovative idea would you propose to solve the local waste challenges? Write down two ideas you are going to propose.

____

____

____

____

____

____

____

____

Sketches:

1. **Symphony of Collaboration**: Illustrate a government official and a CEO shaking hands, with a recycling plant and eco-friendly products in the background.

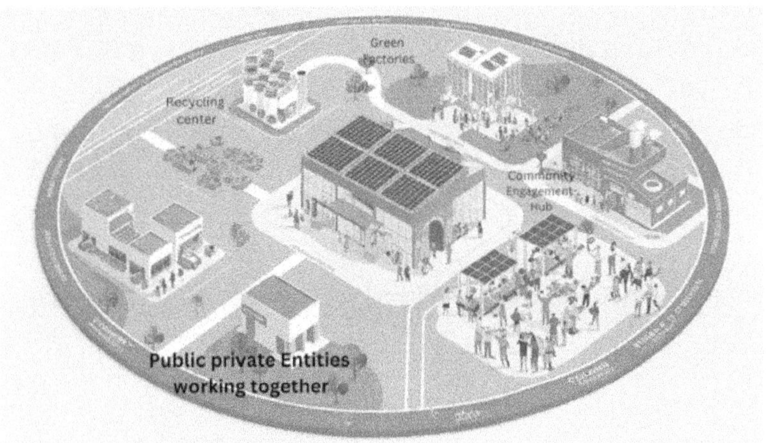

2. **Circular City Map**: A visual of public and private entities working together—recycling centres, green factories, and community engagement hubs.

Public-private partnerships exemplify how collaboration can harmonise the strengths of diverse entities, transforming the dream of a circular economy into a tangible reality.

Call to Action for Policymakers

To understand this part, it is important to know about a story.

A story about a responsible consumer:

Maya is a mindful consumer of the bustling city of Bengaluru. Well-known in her neighbourhood for her eco-conscious ways, Maya always took the extra step of sorting recyclables, fixing appliances when they faltered, and disposing of waste in an environmentally friendly manner. For her, supporting a circular economy was not just a trend—it was a personal commitment to giving old items a new lease on life.

One evening, while preparing for dinner, Maya reached her dependable microwave only to find that it had suddenly stopped working. Refusing to add it to the landfill, she dedicated hours to tinkering with its inner workings, hoping to restore functionality. Despite these efforts, microwaves remained unresponsive. Rather than surrendering to wastefulness, she decided to donate it to a local recycling centre known to revive electronic parts.

Unfortunately, Maya's challenges did not end. In the following weeks, one appliance began to fail after another. First, her cherished music system began to emit odd, garbled sounds. Soon, the induction stove she relied on began acting unpredictably, and eventually, even the geyser that warmed her water gave out. With every new malfunction, Maya's frustration grew as she watched her collection of broken gadgets.

Undeterred by these setbacks, Maya resolved to adhere to her sustainable lifestyle by donating every malfunctioning device to a facility that could repurpose them. However, she soon ran into an unexpected hurdle; the process was simple. Information was scattered across multiple sources; each recycling centre had its own contact details and unique procedures. This disjointed approach left Maya bewildered about whom to call and what steps to take. What should have been an uncomplicated contribution to the circular economy became a confusing maze.

Reflecting on her experience, Maya realised that if a dedicated and informed citizen faced such challenges, many others might abandon their broken appliances altogether.

This insight sparked a vision: Imagine that managing electronic waste was as straightforward as calling the police or ambulance in an emergency.

Picture **a system where a single phone call or a quick tap on a smartphone sets off a chain of actions to safely and efficiently collect broken appliances. Such a solution would require a centralised, government-backed e-waste management platform that unifies all recycling centres under a single, accessible network. Clear guidelines and standardised procedures would remove guesswork, making it easy for everyone to participate in a sustainable circular economy.**

Implementing such a policy can drastically reduce the environmental impact of electronic waste. This would encourage greater participation in recycling efforts, protect our natural resources, and even stimulate the creation of green jobs by facilitating the efficient reuse of valuable components. Maya's experience is a compelling call to action for policymakers: **we need a waste management system that is as intuitive and accessible as emergency services, ensuring that every citizen can contribute to a healthier, more sustainable future.**

Let us urge our governments to embrace this vision—a future in which managing e-waste is no longer a convoluted task but a simple, reliable process accessible to all.

In conclusion, it is imperative that policymakers adopt a framework that ensures the clear and consistent execution of circular practices. Maya's story vividly illustrates how even the most environmentally conscious individuals can be hindered by a disjointed and confusing waste management system. We must urge our leaders to heed this call for change.

Imagine that, much like dialling a number for emergency services, a single call or tap could set in motion the efficient collection and recycling of electronic waste. A centralised, government-backed platform would eliminate the current maze of disparate contacts and procedures, providing every citizen with a straightforward way to participate in the circular economy.

Let us encourage policymakers to develop and implement a system that is as intuitive and accessible as emergency services, ensuring that every broken appliance or outdated device finds its way back into a sustainable loop. The time for fragmented solutions is over; a unified, crystal-clear approach to circular practices is essential for safeguarding the environment and empowering communities to contribute to a greener future.

Recap and Summary:

1. **Importance of Policies:** Government regulations and incentives are crucial for driving the circular economy and ensuring that businesses adopt sustainable practices.

2. **Role of Policy in Circular Transition**: Policies such as tax benefits for eco-friendly businesses, waste management standards, and mandatory recycling laws support circularity, while reducing environmental damage.

3. **Global Success Stories**: Examples include Europe's *Green Deal*, Japan's Home Appliance Recycling Law, and Singapore's *Zero Waste Masterplan*, showcasing effective policies that drive sustainable transitions.

4. **Public-Private Partnerships**: Collaborations between governments and businesses, such as the *Closed-Loop Fund* in the U.S. and India's *EPR framework*, accelerate circular practices by sharing resources and risks.

5. **Long-term Vision**: Policies foster systemic change, inspire innovation, and ensure a future where economic growth aligns with sustainability.

6. **Call to Action for Policymakers**: It is imperative that policymakers adopt a framework that ensures the clear and consistent execution of circular practices.

Government policies are compass guiding society towards a sustainable circular economy.

7

EMPOWERING COMMUNITIES AND INDIVIDUALS IN CIRCULAR PRACTICES

"The circular economy is not just about recycling better. It's about changing our mindset, rethinking how we make and use products, and creating systems that restore, regenerate, and reduce waste."

— Dame Ellen MacArthur

The path to a sustainable future lies in the hands of individuals and communities who possess the capacity to spark transformative change. By equipping people and local groups with information on circular practices, we can stimulate significant progress at the grassroots level. **This chapter explores how everyday actions, informed decisions, and collective efforts can weave the fabric of a circular economy.** By embracing waste reduction, responsible consumption, and encouraging community-driven initiatives, we can rewrite the narrative of resource use. From creating awareness to adopting practical solutions, this chapter demonstrates the profound impact of small, conscious steps in addressing global challenges. It celebrates the role of empowered citizens as catalysts for circular innovation, proving that change begins at home, in neighbourhoods, and within communities. Let us explore in depth the concept of how empowering individuals and communities is valuable for circular practices.

Consumers' Role in Circular Economy: How Demand Drives Change

In a circular economy, **consumers are not just participants but catalysts for transformation. They wield the power of choice and shift markets by prioritising sustainable products and practices.** By increasing consumer awareness and education, consumers can be empowered to make sustainable purchasing decisions. Picture consumers as the wind that propels the sails of a circular ship, steering industries toward innovation and responsibility. Here is how they make a difference:

1. Demand for Transparency and Sustainability

Consumers have the power to demand products according to their choices and shift market demand by prioritising sustainable products and practices. Consumers can search for products that are made from sustainable materials and have minimal packaging and energy efficiency. Production shifts according to demand. Thus, for circular practices, the responsibility shifts towards modern consumers. Modern consumers are increasingly seeking products that are **eco-friendly, recyclable, or responsibly sourced.**

Case Study: Patagonia – Encouraging Sustainability with the "Worn Wear" Programme

Patagonia's "Worn Wear" Programme is a testament to the power of sustainable practices and conscious consumerism. The initiative offers pre-owned, repaired Patagonia clothing to eco-conscious buyers, extending the lifespan of garments and reducing waste.

By promoting repair and reuse, the programme aligns with the growing consumer demand for sustainable options. Regular quality checks ensure that each item meets Patagonia's high standards, thus reinforcing trust in the brand.

Through this initiative, Patagonia not only minimises the environmental impact but also builds a loyal community of consumers who value sustainability and ethical choices.

> **Scientific Evidence:** A Nielsen survey found that 73% of global consumers are willing to change their consumption habits to reduce environmental impact.

2. Adopting Circular Lifestyles

Adopting a circular lifestyle not only helps to limit biodiversity loss by slowing down the use of natural resources and reducing landscape and habitat disruption but also reduces total annual greenhouse gas emissions.

Practices such as renting items, buying second-hand goods, and choosing repairable goods encourage businesses to grab circular models.

Example: Platforms like ThredUp (second-hand clothing) and Rent the Runway (fashion rental) thrive because of consumer interest in sustainable alternatives.

3. Community Engagement and Advocacy

Partnership and community engagement are vital for promoting a circular economy. **Through advocacy and community engagement, they can raise awareness, drive demands for sustainable products and services, and hold companies and governments responsible for their actions.**

Consumers advocating for green policies encourage governments and corporations to adopt circularity.

Practical Scenario: Local communities initiating "zero waste" stores or supporting farmers' markets reduce single-use plastics and food waste.

4. Cultural Shifts and Education

Education and knowledge play critical roles in circular shifts by shaping attitudes, raising awareness, and promoting sustainability practices. Training and self-awareness camps organised by educational institutes, companies, and the government are helpful in shifting.

Knowledge sharing through social media or workshops inspires circular practices and normalises sustainable consumption.

Interactive Prompt: Imagine hosting a community repair café—what items would you fix to reduce waste?

5. Emotional Appeal and Metaphor

Consumers are nothing else but drops of water that together form a mighty river, creating a new path for sustainability. Their everyday choices ripple outward, with policies, influencing industries, and global systems.

Sketch:

A three-panel illustration:

1. A consumer choosing products with eco-labels on a shelf.
2. A bustling thrift store where items find a second life.

3. A family hosting a garage sale, symbolising resource sharing and reuse.

Indeed, consumers play a crucial role in the circular economy by making well-informed decisions. Their thoughtful choices demonstrate that even minor actions can contribute significantly to building a more sustainable world.

Creating Awareness and Educating the Public: Building Foundations for Circularity

Public awareness is the cornerstone of the successful transition to a circular economy. **By fostering understanding and inspiring action, we can create communities that not only participate in circular practices but also advocate for them.** Think of education as a spark that lights a chain reaction of change, igniting curiosity, responsibility, and collaboration. What is the procedure for using education and awareness in circularity, let us understand it one by one.

1. The Power of Storytelling

The stories simplify complex ideas and make them relatable and inspirable. Sharing examples, like the transformation of waste materials into valuable products, involves emotions and promotes understanding.

Documentaries such as *The True Cost* inspire viewers to demand changes through relatable narratives.

2. Leveraging Digital Tools and Campaigns

Currently, it is impossible to do things without the help of digital tools and campaigns. Therefore, proper use of digital media is very important for obtaining massive results. Digital platforms amplify awareness through targeted campaigns.

Social media challenges, like "Plastic Free July," engage millions to adopt small yet impactful changes, creating a ripple effect of sustainable practices.

3. Hands-On Community Workshops

Really, there is a big difference between theory and practice, and we all know if we want to inculcate anything within us; on that time, a practical approach is unavoidable. Thus, hands-on community workshops are helpful in this transition. **Practical experiences deepen our understanding and encourage action.**

Hosting events such as "Fix-It Days," where people learn to repair and upcycle items, build skills, and promote sustainable habits. Studies have shown that experiential learning has a lasting effect.

4. Circular Economy in Schools and Colleges

To create awareness in everyone, it is very important to educate about the importance of the transition at the grassroots level, which is possible only through children's education in schools and colleges. **Integrating circular economic concepts into education creates a knowledgeable and proactive generation.**

Countries such as Finland lead by including sustainability in their school curricula and preparing students for a circular future.

5. Public-Private Collaboration for Campaigns

For any initiative that is important for change, the involvement of everyone is very important. If they are engaged for the same purpose, they try to understand each other instead of pulling their legs. In this transition, changes were required in old beliefs and practices. Thus, unitedly, it will work. **Businesses and governments can unite to spread awareness effectively.**

Campaigns like Coca-Cola's "World Without Waste" combine reach and resources to educate and inspire action on recycling and reuse.

6. Emotional Appeal and Metaphor

Essentially, consciousness serves as the foundation for a flourishing sustainability movement, with education strengthening its base and disseminating information far and wide. Each person possesses the capability to foster this development.

Sketch:

A four-panel illustration:

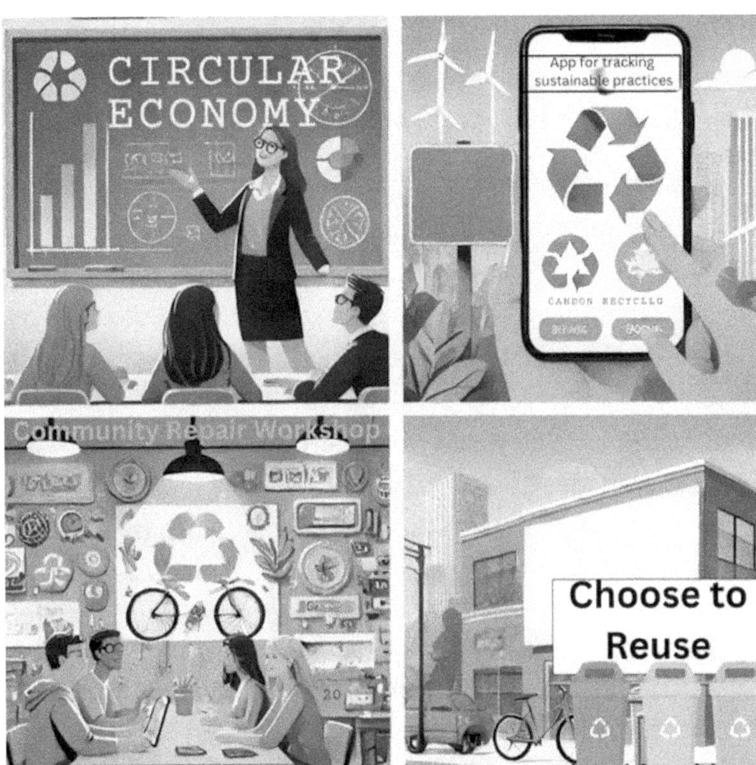

1. A teacher explaining circular economy concepts to a classroom.
2. A smartphone screen showing an app for tracking sustainable practices.
3. A community repair workshop bustling with activity.
4. A billboard featuring a campaign like "Choose to Reuse" alongside recycling bins.

By promoting understanding and providing knowledge, we convert passive onlookers into engaged contributors, revealing the capacity for communities to lead the charge in circular economy initiatives.

Everyday Circular Actions: Simple Steps Towards a Circular Economy

"A journey of a thousand miles begins with a single step," Really this is the right proverb in this context. Taking small steps towards a desired goal is key to achieving the goal. Here, our goal is to transition from a linear economy to a circular economy. Therefore, **every individual has the power to convert the tide of waste and overconsumption.** Everyday actions, no matter how small, ripple outward to create lasting changes. Think of it as a daily act of guardianship: choosing wisely, using thoughtfully, and sharing generously. Let us understand these small changes that resulted in massive results.

1. Responsible Consumption

Responsible consumption in this regard means such a type of consumption that reduces waste and environmental impact and creates a more sustainable future. **By prioritising durable and sustainable products, consumers can reduce the waste at their sources.** For example, choosing a refillable glass water bottle over a single-use plastic eliminates numerous disposable bottles from the waste stream.

> Scientific studies have shown that using a product for an additional six months can reduce its environmental impact by 20-30%.

This is now a question for you. Are you working on responsible consumption? How and What is this? Jot down below:

____

____

____

____

____

____

____

2. Reuse and Repair

Instead of throwing things that are no longer needed, let us consider alternative ways to prolong their lives. Repairing means discarding fewer products; therefore, less pollution and fewer new products. **Repair and reuse extend the life of items and reduce the demand for new resources.** Community repair workshops or "fix-it" cafes foster collaboration and skill-sharing.

Case in point: Sweden's tax incentives for repair services encourage citizens to choose to fix over replacement.

3. Reducing Waste

Reducing the amount of waste creation not only helps to prevent pollution, but also limits the amount of waste going to landfills, preserves natural resources, and saves money. Simple practices, such as opting for reusable shopping bags, composting kitchen scraps, and saying no to single-use plastics, can dramatically reduce waste.

For instance, composting can divert up to 30% of household waste from landfills, while enriching soil for gardens.

4. Recycling Done Right

Recycling is the process of collecting and processing materials that would otherwise be discarded as trash and turning them into new products. **Recycling can benefit the economy, community, and environment.** Recycling is not only about tossing items into a bin; it requires thoughtful sorting to avoid contamination. Local recycling guides were used to maximise the effectiveness.

Cities such as San Francisco have achieved over 80% waste diversion through community education.

5. The sharing economy

The sharing economy is an economic model that works on the sharing of unutilised assets or skills, often facilitated through online platforms. **The sharing economy allows individuals to access goods and services without owning them outright, promoting a more efficient use of resources and reducing waste.** Sharing and borrowing items instead of owning everything individually can reduce unnecessary purchases.

Tools libraries and peer-to-peer platforms like "BorrowMyStuff" exemplify this approach.

6. Second-hand Shopping

Second-hand shopping is a key part of a circular economy because it helps provide affordable options, maintain product value, reduce environmental impact, and support local economies. In fact, reuse prolongs the lifespan of a product.

Purchasing the second-hand puts these things back into circulation, reducing their overall environmental footprint. Thrift stores, online marketplaces, and clothing swaps provide items a second life.

Patagonia's "Worn Wear" Programme repairs and resells used gear, promoting circular fashion.

Interactive Scenario

Now, it is your turn. Imagine you are organising a birthday party. Could you:

- Borrow decorations and utensils from neighbours.
- Compost food scraps.
- Encouraging guests to bring gifts to reusable packaging.

Sketch:

A three-panel illustration:

1. **Responsible Shopping:** A consumer picking a product with a "Made Sustainably" label.

2. **Sharing Culture:** Neighbours exchanging tools at a local sharing library.
3. **Creative Reuse:** A family repurposing jars as plant pots.

Through the adoption of these straightforward yet effective strategies, individuals become ambassadors of the circular economy, paving the way for a more sustainable tomorrow.

Recap and Summary:

1. **Consumer Role in the Circular Economy:**

   a. Consumers drive demand for sustainable products by choosing eco-friendly and circular options.
   b. Case studies show how consumer preferences push businesses to innovate toward sustainability.

2. **Creating Awareness and Educating the Public:**

   a. Educating communities fosters a culture of sustainability.
   b. Strategies include workshops, apps for tracking sustainable habits, and campaigns like "Choose to Reuse."

3. **Circular actions every day:**

   a. Simple actions such as buying second-hand goods, repairing goods, and reducing waste empowers individuals.
   b. Real-life examples highlight how small collective steps lead to significant changes.

Empowering individuals and communities form the foundation of a circular economy. This chapter emphasises the significance of consumer choices, the role of awareness, and actionable steps, showcasing how everyone can contribute to sustainable prosperity.

8

MEASURING AND TRACKING CIRCULAR ECONOMY IMPACT

"What gets measured gets managed."
— Peter Drucker

Measurement is a technique in which the properties of an object are determined by comparing them with a standard quantity. Without measurements, we could not determine the success rate. Actually, here measurement is the compass that guides the journey toward a circular economy, and establishing progress aligns with intent. Tracking impact is the cornerstone of success in a world in which sustainability demands accountability.

The eighth chapter examines the key performance indicators, crucial instruments, and response systems that measure circular methodologies and connect aspirations with practical insights. **This chapter unpacks from key performance indicators** like waste reduction and resource recovery rates to advanced tools like life-cycle assessments, and how data drives innovation. By encouraging continuous assessment and improvement, we can transform the circular economy not only from vision to measurable reality but also prove that prosperity and sustainability go hand in hand.

Key Performance Indicators for Circularity

Measuring the effects of circular economy requires precise instruments, similar to how a navigator uses a compass to guide through unexplored seas. **Circularity Key Performance Indicators (KPIs) serve as quantitative measures of advancement, establishing that initiatives produce measurable outcomes. These standards assist companies, government officials, and individuals in evaluating the success of eco-friendly practices.** Let us now understand the different key performance indicators of circularity.

1. Waste Reduction: Measuring What We Save

Key performance indicators (KPIs) for waste reduction monitoring and evaluation of the number of materials saved from landfills through sustainable practices, such as reuse and recycling. This measurement not only showcases current achievements but also pinpoints opportunities for future enhancement.

For example, IKEA's commitment to a circular economy diverted 90% of its operational waste through reuse and recycling.

Scientific Insight: According to the UNEP, scaling circular practices globally could reduce waste generation by half, save resources, and kerb environmental harm.

2. Resource Recovery Rate: Mining from Waste

This performance indicator assesses the proportion of materials salvaged from previously used products and reintegrated into economic processes. This underscores the effectiveness of recycling operations and encourages resource self-sufficiency by minimising dependence on new raw materials.

- **Case Study**: Dell's "closed-loop" recycling programme reclaims plastics from old electronics to manufacture new devices, illustrating how businesses can convert waste into valuable inputs.
- **Interactive Scenario**: Imagine designing a car. How could resource recovery maximise the reuse of metals, plastics, and electronics after its lifecycle.

3. Carbon Footprint: The Climate Connection

Key performance indicators (KPIs) for carbon footprints offer a measurable assessment of greenhouse gas emissions throughout a product or process's lifecycle. **These indicators highlight areas with high emissions, prompting efforts to minimise environmental impacts.**

- **For example**, Adidas reduced its sneaker emissions by 30% using recycled ocean plastics, proving that sustainable materials have significant climatic benefits.

- **Scientific Evidence**: A report by the Ellen MacArthur Foundation revealed that adopting circular practices could cut global emissions by 39%, addressing climate change directly.

Key Performance Indicators (KPIs) represent more than mere statistics; they narrate our dedication to sustainability. These metrics offer transparency, responsibility, and motivation, demonstrating that our progress towards a circular economy is quantifiable, significant, and within reach. By adopting these measurements, we transform our goals into concrete actions.

Tools and Frameworks: Unlocking the Circular Economy

A circular economy is an economic model that aims to keep materials in use, eliminate waste and pollution, and regenerate natural systems. In fact, navigating the circular economy is like assembling a puzzle; each piece requires alignment and precision. **Tools and frameworks serve as guidebooks** offering clarity, consistency, and direction for measuring progress. From life-cycle assessments (LCA) to carbon accounting, these methodologies ensure that actions align with sustainability goals. Let us individually understand these tools and frameworks.

1. Life-Cycle Assessments (LCA): The Full Story of a Product

LCA is the process of evaluating the effects of a product on the environment over the entire period of its life, thereby increasing resource use efficiency and decreasing liabilities. LCAs evaluate a product's environmental impact across its entire lifecycle: raw material extraction, production, usage, and disposal. Businesses can focus on reducing their ecological footprints by identifying the most resource-intensive stages.

For example, Unilever used LCAs to improve the sustainability of dove-soap bars by focusing on water and energy conservation.

Sketch:

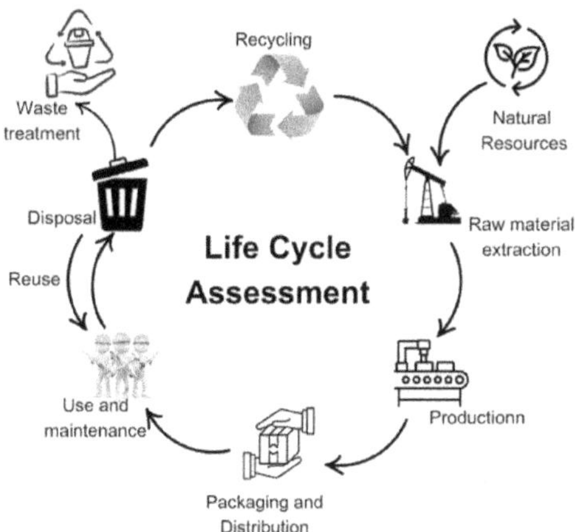

LCA: A timeline of a product, from raw material to disposal.

2. Carbon Accounting: Tracking the Invisible Pollutant

The measurement of greenhouse gas emissions for various processes, known as carbon accounting, offers a comprehensive view of an organisation's environmental impact. The Greenhouse Gas Protocol outlines two primary approaches: spend-based and activity-based. This accounting practice identifies areas of high emissions, allowing for focused efforts to reduce them. Individuals, businesses, and governments rely on carbon accounting to measure and control greenhouse gas emissions, facilitating targeted actions for reduction. This tool is essential for understanding and managing the carbon footprints associated with different activities and processes.

Microsoft exemplifies this by rigorously tracking supply chain emissions to meet carbon neutrality goals.

3. Circularity Gap Reporting: Bridging the Divide

Governments can utilise Circularity Gap Reports to understand the most impactful strategies for enhancing circularity at the national and regional levels, establishing objectives, and tracking advancements. **These reports evaluate the proportion of an economy functioning based on circular principles and identify specific areas that require improvement.**

The 2023 Circularity Gap Report revealed that only 8.6% of the global economy is circular, underscoring the potential for significant progress in resource recovery and reuse.

4. Material Flow Analysis (MFA): Tracking Resource Journeys

Material Flow Analysis (MFA) tracks how resources move within a system, highlighting inefficient processes and potential areas for material reuse. The circularity rate indicates the proportion of recycled materials reintroduced into the economy compared to the overall material consumption, thereby decreasing the need to extract new raw materials. This metric encompasses the movement of materials, fossil fuels and energy products.

Amsterdam's city-wide circular strategy relies on MFA to optimise construction material usage and manage organic waste streams effectively.

These tools provide essential metrics and evaluations to track progress and develop plans for a sustainable future, helping organisations and governments align their efforts with the principles of a circular economy.

Feedback Loops for Improvement

In a circular economy, feedback loops function as vital mechanisms, similar to how a cyclist constantly adjusts to maintain balance on a curvy path. **These loops involve the reintegration of used materials, waste, and by-products into manufacturing processes, which helps reduce environmental impact and the need for raw resource extraction.** By fostering efficiency, facilitating ongoing resource circulation, and lessening reliance on the linear "extract-produce-discard" model, feedback loops play a crucial role in promoting sustainability within circular economic systems.

They asserted that errors are corrected, progress is monitored, and practices evolve. Circular systems flourish on iterative learning, where each cycle offers insights that refine the next.

1. The Role of Feedback Loops in Progress

Feedback loops allow businesses and policymakers to evaluate the impact of their circular initiatives and make necessary adjustments. By regularly measuring KPIs such as waste reduction and resource recovery, organisations can identify bottlenecks and optimise their systems.

  a. **Example**: Unilever's sustainable packaging initiative uses feedback loops to improve materials based on customer usage data, reducing waste by 50% in select markets.
  b. **Interactive Scenario**: Imagine a clothing brand monitoring repair and resale rates. Data from customers reveals trends, enabling them to design more durable and desirable products.

2. Scientific Insights on Adaptive Systems

Feedback is essential for the success of an adaptive system. Research in the field of system dynamics demonstrates that well-functioning feedback mechanisms minimise inefficiencies, enhance system resilience, and foster innovation.

  c. **Scientific Evidence**: Research from MIT shows that companies employing iterative learning cycles in sustainability efforts achieve 20–30% higher resource efficiency than static approaches.

3. Practical Examples of Continuous Improvement

Case Study: Renault – Innovating Efficiency with Remanufacturing

Renault's remanufacturing plant in France sets a benchmark for sustainable production by reusing materials and cutting waste. The plant uses real-time feedback from production lines to identify inefficiencies and optimise processes.

This approach has enabled Renault to reduce raw material consumption by 80% compared to traditional manufacturing methods. By integrating technology and sustainability, the plant not only lowers environmental impact but also enhances operational efficiency.

Renault's model demonstrates how innovation in remanufacturing can drive significant resource savings while supporting a circular economy.

Metaphor: Think of a GPS recalibrating your route after every incorrect turn. Feedback loops guide circular systems in the same way, ensuring that goals are achieved despite the challenges.

4. Technology as an Enabler

Real-time data and transparency are provided by cutting-edge technologies, such as the Internet of Things (IoT) and blockchain, which improve feedback systems.

example, Walmart leverages blockchain to track food supply chains, enabling swift adjustments to reduce waste and ensure product freshen.

Sketch:

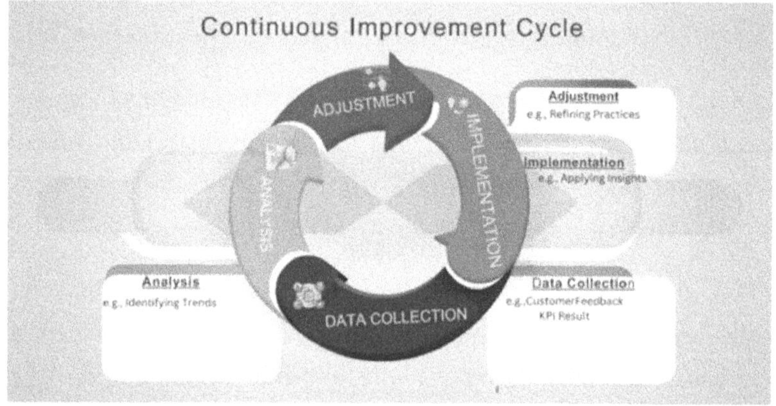

- A looped flowchart illustrating:

   o **Data Collection** (e.g., customer feedback, KPI results) → **Analysis** (e.g., identifying trends) → **Adjustment** (e.g., refining practices) → **Implementation** (e.g., applying insights).

Feedback loops transform a circular economy into a dynamically evolving system. By embracing constant evaluation and refinement, businesses and communities can stay ahead of challenges, continually innovate, and accelerate their transition toward sustainability. Each iteration brings us closer to a world where nothing is wasted and everything holds a value.

Recap and Summary:

1. **Key Performance Indicators (KPIs) for Circularity:**

   a. Metrics such as waste reduction, resource recovery rate, carbon footprint, and life-cycle assessment (LCA) provide measurable insights into the success of circular initiatives.

    b. Examples include IKEA's waste reduction and Dell's closed-loop recycling programmes, which showcase tangible progress.

    c. These KPIs help businesses and policymakers ensure accountability and refine their sustainability efforts.

2. **Tools and Frameworks for Measurement:**

    a. Life-cycle assessments (LCA) and carbon accounting are essential tools for evaluating environmental impacts.

    b. Case studies such as Patagonia's use of LCA for sustainable fabrics highlight how businesses can leverage these frameworks for better decisions.

    c. Digital platforms enhance tracking and reporting capabilities and promote transparency.

3. **Feedback Loops for Improvement:**

    a. Continuous assessment and adjustment fuelled by feedback loops enable adaptive and resilient circular systems.

    b. Examples such as Unilever's packaging improvements and Renault's remanufacturing emphasise the importance of iteration.

    c. Technologies such as IoT and blockchain ensure real-time tracking and efficient recalibration.

This chapter emphasises the importance of measurement and adaptation as the backbone of circular progress. **These tools empower stakeholders to innovate, evolve, and remain aligned with sustainability goals.**

9

OVERCOMING CHALLENGES IN THE CIRCULAR TRANSITION

"We cannot solve our problems with the same thinking we used when we created them."

— Albert Einstein

"The path to a circular economy is not a straightforward journey but a challenging ascent. Every obstacle we encounter—whether economic, regulatory, or cultural—is an opportunity to rethink, redesign, and reimagine the way we live, consume, and coexist with our planet."

If you want to make changes in any aspect, even for betterment, it is not easy. To accept any changes, it is important to train your mind, especially your subconscious mind, that this change is not only important but inevitable. Without this, you cannot even think about the survival of our planet.

The journey towards a circular economy has obstacles because many changes are required in our consumption and production patterns. Regulatory complexities, economic expenditure, and cultural remonstrance often stand in the way of progress. However, these obstacles are merely disguised opportunities for collaboration, education, and innovation. This section examines the difficulties communities, businesses, and governments face as they move towards a circular economy. **By addressing these barriers through strategies such as partnerships, technological progress, and incentive programmes, we pave the way for sustainable development. Surmounting these challenges is not just about perseverance; it is also about reimagining possibilities and securing a thriving future within the limits of our planet's resources.**

Addressing Common Obstacles in the Circular Transition

The transition to a circular economy presents both opportunities and significant obstacles. **The journey towards**

sustainability is impeded by various challenges, including financial burdens, legislative impediments, and societal reluctance to change. These barriers can be likened to the demanding stages of an enduring race. To successfully navigate these hurdles, a combination of strategic planning, unwavering determination, and collaborative effort is essential. In the following sections, we delve into crucial strategies for addressing these impediments.

1. Economic Costs: Bridging the Gap Between Vision and Viability

Shifting to circular economic models typically requires substantial initial investment in innovation, product redesign, and new infrastructure. Nevertheless, these upfront expenditures are offset by the long-term benefits of resource conservation and the increased resilience of the system.

- **Example**: Unilever's switch to 100% recycled plastic packaging initially raised costs but led to a 15% reduction in raw material expenses within three years.

- **Scientific Insight**: A McKinsey report highlights that circular strategies can unlock $4.5 trillion in global economic benefits by 2030.

- **Practical Scenario**: Imagine a startup choosing between cheaper linear production or investing in recyclable materials, which is a trade-off with future payoffs.

2. Regulatory Barriers: Aligning Policies for Progress

Circular economy adoption can be impeded by outdated or inconsistent regulations that often favour traditional linear economic models. **Legal and financial obstacles may hamper**

the development of circular economies. One example is the absence of well-defined property rights in waste management, which can discourage businesses from investing in recycling and waste management infrastructures. It is very important to remove these barriers for a better future. **Collaborative policymaking is essential for driving change.**

Case Study: India – Managing E-Waste with Responsible Practices

The E-Waste Management Rules introduced in India in 2016 have been a game-changer for addressing electronic waste. These regulations require manufacturers to take responsibility for collecting and recycling e-waste through an Extended Producer Responsibility (EPR) framework.

By formalising the recycling process, the initiative encouraged the development of proper facilities and reduced the environmental impact of discarded electronics. Public awareness and regular reviews have ensured their effectiveness.

This framework not only minimises e-waste but also promotes a culture of accountability and sustainable resource use among manufacturers and consumers.

Example: The EU's Circular Economy Action Plan streamlined policies, enabling businesses to integrate circularity seamlessly.

Interactive Element: What policy changes could accelerate recycling in a city? Brainstorms and comparison with global examples.

3. Cultural Resistance: Shifting Mindsets Toward Circular Practices

There is a belief in our mind that everything that is going on is good, and there is no need to change it. Such type of resistance comes into our mind due to ingrained habits, values, and norms. Because of this, individuals and society are reluctant to adopt sustainable and circular approaches. **There is a requirement for education, awareness, and incentives to reframe perceptions to overcome this and foster the acceptance of eco-friendly behaviours and practices for long-term sustainability. Cultural habits and perceptions often resisted unfamiliarity. Engaging communities with education and incentives helps break these barriers and achieve massive results.**

Example: Public campaigns and school programmes have ingrained Japan's "*Mottainai*" culture of avoiding waste.

Metaphors: Like a river carved through stones, gradual education reshapes societal norms.

Sketch:

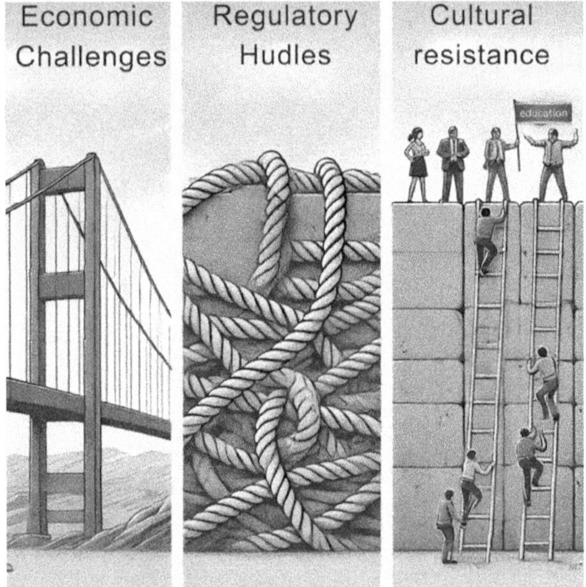

- Three barriers visualised:

  o A high-cost bridge labelled "Economic Challenges."
  o A tangled rope labelled "Regulatory Hurdles."
  o A wall labelled "Cultural Resistance" with people climbing it, aided by education banners.

By addressing these challenges head-on, we pave the way for a resilient and sustainable circular economy, transforming obstacles into stepping stones for a better tomorrow.

Strategies for Mitigation in the Circular Transition

Transitioning to a circular economy, such as climbing a mountain, is challenging now, but after reaching the destination, it is rewarding. To reach a summit, we need strategies that address the steep hurdles of regulatory gaps, economic constraints, and cultural inertia. **Strategies for mitigation play an important role in the transition to a circular economy.** These strategies aim to reduce the negative social, environmental, and economic impacts during the transformation from a linear to a circular system. Mitigation strategies ensure that the transition to a circular economy is sustainable, equitable, and effective, minimising challenges and maximising benefits for all stakeholders. Innovation incentives, strategic partnerships, and consumer education are ropes and ladders for overcoming these hurdles. Let us understand how helpful this is.

1. Innovation Incentives: Fuelling Creative Solutions

Think about a child who is not willing to study but is ready to know that reward will be given after completing the study. The child agreed to do so and finished it within time. Similarly, innovation incentives work in a circular economy. **Innovation incentives refer to mechanisms or factors that motivate organisations and individuals to develop new products, ideas, or processes. Organisations and Governments can offer grants, subsidies, and tax breaks to encourage businesses to develop circular innovation. These incentives reduce the financial burden associated with adopting sustainable practices.**

Case Study: Sweden – Incentivising Circular Practices with Repair Tax Rebates

Sweden promotes circular practices by offering tax breaks for businesses and individuals who prioritise sustainability. A standout initiative is the repair tax rebate, which reduces the cost of repairing items like clothing and electronics.

This approach encourages reuse, cuts waste, and supports a more sustainable economy while making eco-friendly choices accessible to everyone.

- **Example:** The European Innovation Council funds startups focused on circular solutions such as biodegradable materials and efficient recycling technologies.

- **Scientific Evidence:** A 2021 OECD report found that countries offering green innovation subsidies saw a 20% higher adoption rate of circular practices.

- **Practical Scenario:** Picture a small enterprise creating compostable coffee pods but struggling with costs. A government grant bridges this gap by making sustainable products viable.

2. Partnerships: Harnessing the Power of Collaboration

One flower does not make a garland; this proverb also applies to this transition, which is only possible through partnerships among stakeholders.

When governments, corporations, and local communities join forces, they create a synergy that maximises their effectiveness by combining their respective assets, expertise, and reach.

Case Study: Ellen MacArthur Foundation – Building Collaboration Through the Circular Economy 100

The Ellen MacArthur Foundation's Circular Economy 100 (CE100) initiative brings together diverse groups of corporations, NGOs, and academic institutions to design and implement circular solutions. By fostering collaboration, the programme enables participants to share insights, co-develop innovative ideas, and drive systemic change.

This initiative has become a global platform for exchanging knowledge and accelerating the transition to a circular economy. Through partnerships and real-world applications, CE100 empowers its members to create sustainable business models that reduce waste and promote resource efficiency, thus setting a strong example of collective impact.

- **Example**: Coca-Cola partnered with Veolia to build infrastructure for bottle-to-bottle recycling in developing regions, ensuring a steady supply of recycled materials.
- **Metaphor**: Partnerships are like threads in a tapestry; each adds strength and beauty, weaving a sustainable future.

3. Consumer Education: Transforming Awareness into Action

Nelson Mandela said," Education is the most powerful weapon you can use to change the world." This quote is correct in every aspect. Thus, **consumer education helps transform awareness into action and achieve the desired result. It is very important to make consumers aware of the right** actions that help achieve a circular economy.

Empowering individuals through campaigns, workshops, and school programmes builds a culture of conscious consumption and waste reduction.

Example: Sweden's "Repair Café" initiative teaches citizens how to fix items rather than discard them, reducing waste and fostering a community.

Interactive Content: An app gamifies sustainable choices, rewarding users for recycling or buying second-hand goods, creating a ripple effect of change.

Sketch:

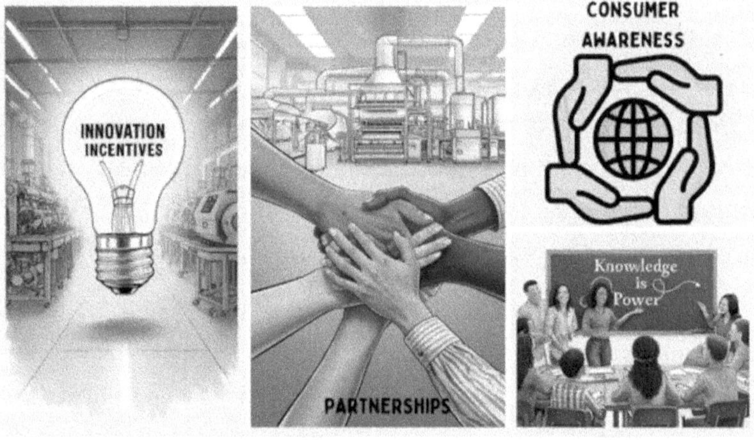

- **Panel 1**: A lightbulb labelled "Innovation Incentives" illuminating a factory producing sustainable goods.
- **Panel 2**: Diverse hands clasped, representing partnerships, with industries and communities in the background.
- **Panel 3**: A teacher explaining circular economy to students, with "Knowledge is Power" on a blackboard.

With these strategies, the journey to a circular economy becomes achievable. Each incentive, partnership, and lesson learned chips away at resistance, transforming the mountain into a path forward.

Role of Technology and Innovation in Circular Transition

Technology and innovation power the circular economy, like spacecraft navigating humanity to a sustainable future. Technology plays a role in implementing design principles that focus on creating more accessible products to disassemble, repair, and recycle that adhere to the principle of a circular economy right from their initial stages.

Breakthroughs in material science and cutting-edge digital solutions enable a shift from linear to circular practices, reducing waste, optimising resource use, and creating new economic opportunities. Let us deep dive into it.

1. Material Science: Building the Foundations of Circularity

Materials science investigates materials' characteristics, creation, and usage to promote sustainable advancement. This discipline supports circular economy concepts by creating long-lasting, reusable, and efficient materials, encouraging closed-loop processes, and minimising environmental consequences. Consequently, material science contributes to developing a sustainable, adaptable, and waste-minimising future.

Innovations in materials science pave the way for eco-friendly substitutes for conventional resources, enhancing the effectiveness of recycling and reuse processes. Developing compostable plastics, self-repairing materials, and repurposed textiles is transforming the various industrial sectors.

Case Study: LanzaTech – Turning Emissions into Opportunities

LanzaTech has revolutionised sustainability by using microbes to transform industrial emissions into ethanol. These microbes capture carbon-rich gases from factories and convert them into valuable resources that serve as building blocks for fuel, chemicals, and other products.

This innovative process not only reduces greenhouse gas emissions, but also creates sustainable alternatives to traditional raw materials. By blending cutting-edge science with environmental responsibility, LanzaTech showcases how industrial waste can be turned into a resource, offering a scalable solution for a cleaner and greener future.

> **Scientific Evidence**: Studies show that bio-based materials can reduce lifecycle emissions by up to 50%, significantly reducing global carbon footprints.

Metaphors: These innovations act as alchemists, transforming waste into gold.

2. Digital Tracking: The GPS of Circular Practices

Modern technology, including blockchain, IoT, and AI, enables digital tracking to monitor items, materials, and processes throughout their lifespans. This approach enhances visibility, maximises resource utilisation, and facilitates reuse, recycling, and waste minimisation. It is a guiding mechanism to enhance productivity and responsibility in circular economic initiatives. Digital tracking functions as a GPS system for circular practice.

Digital tools like blockchain and IoT enable precise tracking of materials and products, ensuring transparency and accountability in supply chains.

- **Example**: IBM's Food Trust uses blockchain to trace the journey of producing and reducing food waste by identifying inefficiencies.
- **Interactive Scenario**: Imagine scanning a QR code on a product to learn its origin, composition, and recyclability, empowering informed choices.

> - **Fact**: A McKinsey report estimated that digital tools can enhance material efficiency by up to 30%, saving billions annually.

3. AI and Automation: Unlocking New Possibilities

Integrating artificial intelligence and automation transforms industries, boosting productivity, minimising waste, and facilitating intelligent choices. These technologies enable proactive maintenance, enhance resource distribution, and refine manufacturing processes. **In a circular economy, AI and automation have paved the way for cutting-edge approaches to recycling, remanufacturing, and eco-friendly practices.** This fosters adaptability and propels advancement towards a more sustainable world.

AI technology enhances various processes, including classifying recyclable materials, forecasting resource requirements, and creating products with modular design.

Example: AMP Robotics developed AI-powered systems that identify and sort recyclables with 98% accuracy, revolutionising waste management.

Scenario: Consider a factory in which robotic arms disassemble electronics for recycling and recover rare Earth metals for reuse.

Sketch:

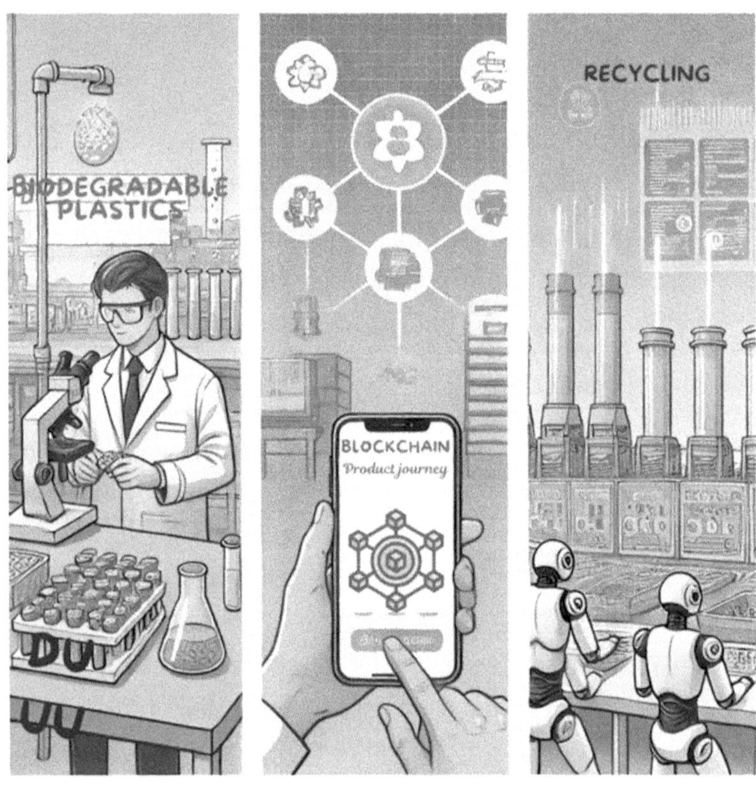

- **Panel 1**: A scientist in a lab creating biodegradable plastics.
- **Panel 2**: A smartphone showing the digital journey of a product via blockchain.
- **Panel 3**: Robots efficiently sorting recyclables in a futuristic facility.

Technology is the compass guiding the circular economy forward, bridging ambition with action. Each breakthrough in material science, digital tracking, or AI fuels the journey, proving that innovation is key to unlocking a sustainable, circular future.

Recap and Summary:

1. Addressing Common Obstacles:

    i. Common obstacles, such as economic costs, regulatory barriers, and cultural resistance, hinder the adoption of circular practices. Addressing these issues is, therefore, essential.

    ii. Case studies, such as India's e-waste recycling struggles, highlight the need for systemic change.

2. Strategies for Mitigation:

    iii. Innovation incentives, public-private partnerships, and consumer education are strategies for mitigation that can counter challenges.

    iv. Examples include tax breaks for circular businesses and programmes like Sweden's repair tax rebates.

3. Role of Technology and Innovation:

    v. Advancements in material science, blockchain technology, and AI are possible only through technology and innovation that enable seamless circular transitions.

    vi. Case studies of companies, such as IBM Food Trust and AMP Robotics, demonstrate transformative potential.

Conclusion: Transitioning into a circular economy requires active steps to address these challenges. **By working together, developing new solutions, and implementing targeted approaches, we can overcome these obstacles and create an economy that is both sustainable and adaptable.**

10

VISION FOR A CIRCULAR FUTURE

"The future depends on what we do in the present."

— Mahatma Gandhi

"Progress is impossible without change, and those who cannot change their minds cannot change anything."

— George Bernard Shaw

Envision a future in which waste no longer exists, resources are continuously reused, and societies flourish in balance with the environment. This section explores the revolutionary potential of a completely circular economy, an approach that combines innovation with sustainability to promote economic resilience, ecological restoration, and social prosperity. By examining concrete advantages, motivating case studies, and practical implementation methods, we present an optimistic outlook on what lies ahead.

This vision can be realised through cooperative efforts between individuals, corporations, and governmental bodies. The chapter ends by urging readers to take action, encouraging them to adopt and promote circular economy principles in both their personal and professional spheres.

The Path to a Fully Circular Economy

A fully circular economy is how much soothing is completely understood by us. If imagination is so great, then what will happen after achieving it?

Imagine a world where waste is obsolete—a place where every product, from your morning coffee cup to the skyscrapers that define cityscapes, is part of a regenerative loop. The vision of a fully circular economy is not utopian; it is a blueprint for sustainable prosperity. Transitioning to such a future requires systemic transformation rooted in innovation, collaboration, and shared commitment. Let us understand what the requirement for fully circular economy is.

1. Eliminating Waste: A World Without Landfills

A completely circular economy converts waste into a valuable resource that can be reintegrated into production. This approach creates systems where all materials are either reused, recycled, or converted into compost, instead of eliminating the necessity for waste disposal methods, such as landfills and incineration.

Countries like Sweden exemplify this by sending less than 1% of household waste to landfills through robust recycling and energy recovery initiatives.

2. A Regenerative Industrial Revolution

Companies are revolutionising their industries by creating circular systems in which waste products become inputs for new manufacturing processes. This innovative approach allows businesses to simultaneously minimise their environmental footprint and enhance their financial performance and operational efficiency.

For example, Interface Carpets produce tiles from recycled materials, demonstrating how circular processes can dramatically lower carbon footprints while meeting consumer demands.

3. Localised Production and Sharing Economies

Local repair centres, resource sharing initiatives, and community-based energy projects are the key components of decentralised systems. These approaches promote self-sufficient communities that reduce the need for long-distance resource transportation and minimise waste generation.

Amsterdam's circular neighbourhoods showcase repair cafes, shared energy grids, and local production, proving the potential of localised economies to thrive sustainably.

4. Technology-Driven Circularity

Cutting-edge technologies, such as artificial intelligence, the Internet of Things, and blockchain, facilitate effective monitoring and visibility of resources, guaranteeing responsibility throughout the process.

Platforms like Circularise showcase how digital tools streamline resource flows, allowing industries to maximise material recovery and minimise waste in real-time

Technology acts as the "neural network" of a circular world, connecting resources that are needed seamlessly.

5. Cultural Shifts Toward Sustainability

Promoting circular thinking requires educational initiatives and public awareness campaigns. A shift in societal values toward conserving resources and embracing sustainable practices is crucial for this transformation.

By adopting philosophies like Japan's *"Mottainai,"* which emphasises minimising waste, communities worldwide can integrate circular principles into everyday life through education and grassroots campaigns.

Sketch:

- A vibrant cityscape:

o Zero waste zones.

o Solar panels and green rooftops.

o People using apps to swap goods, sharing bikes, and repairing products at community hubs.

By embracing circular principles, we create a world that celebrates regeneration, reduces environmental harm, and ensures prosperity for all. This vision is not just achievable; it is essential for humanity's future.

Long-Term Benefits of Circularity

It is now time to consider the long-term benefits of a circular economy. It is nothing other than planting a seed today that grows into a fruitful tree. If more seeds are planted, they become vigorous, constructive forests for future generations, which only benefit them.

The concept of a circular economy presents a compelling vision: a sustainable cycle in which ecosystems prosper, resources are preserved, and communities thrive. Moreover, it has the potential to deliver such promises. By incorporating circular principles into economic, environmental, and social frameworks, we can cultivate a world that prioritises balance over excess consumption. Therefore, it is crucial to consider the long-term advantages of circularity. Let us ponder it.

1. Economic Stability and Resilience

A circular economy can achieve financial stability and resilience. **It reduces dependency on finite resources and promotes local industries, minimising supply chain disruptions and building resilience.**

For example, a 2021 study by Accenture estimated that adopting circular models could unlock $4.5 trillion in global economic opportunities by 2030. Countries like Denmark have embraced circularity to reduce resource dependence and boost economic security.

Interactive Scenario: Now, it is time for you to imagine a factory that reuses materials indefinitely. How might this affect costs, innovation, and jobs over the decades? Only such thinking gives us the energy to adopt a circular economy and redesign our prosperity.

2. Environmental Regeneration

Circularity regenerates natural systems, allowing ecosystems to restore themselves while reducing pollution and waste. **The circular economy addresses critical issues like biodiversity loss by prioritising renewable resources and sustainable production.** The Ellen MacArthur Foundation highlights how circular agriculture practices, such as agroforestry, enhance soil fertility and carbon sequestration.

   a. **Example:** The Netherlands recycles 80% of construction waste, reducing resource extraction and land degradation.

3. Societal Well-Being

Circularity improves quality of life not only through sustainable consumption and cleaner environments, but also by equitable access to resources. Shared mobility, community repair workshops, and sustainable housing initiatives promote inclusivity and collaboration. In India, urban mining projects extract materials from e-waste, creating jobs and reducing landfill dependency.

   b. **Metaphor:** A circular society is like a well-tuned orchestra, where every element works harmoniously to create lasting beauty.

4. Cultural Legacy for Future Generations

A completely circular economy fosters principles of responsible management, innovation, and environmental

consciousness in future generations, providing a cultural legacy for them.

Educational institutions in Finland incorporate circular economy concepts through practical, hands-on learning experiences, enabling students to develop innovative solutions with a focus on responsibility.

Sketch:

- Green factories with "zero waste" banners.
- A thriving cityscape powered by renewable energy.
- A family planting trees with "circular future" written in the soil.

By weaving circularity into our systems, we create a future marked by abundance, resilience, and equity—a world where economic growth does not come at the expense of nature or humanity but works in tandem with both.

Call to Action: Be Champions of the Circular Economy

The circular economy is more than just an idea—it is a transformative movement that relies on collaborative effort. Each person can influence the future, similar to how individual water droplets combine to create a powerful ocean. Now is your opportunity to emerge as an agent of change, integrating circularity into both your career and personal activities. By adopting eco-friendly practices, promoting systemic shifts, and motivating others, you can contribute to developing a robust, fair, and prosperous world.

1. Individual Actions Have Ripple Effects

Individuals can promote a circular economy by taking steps, such as reducing consumption and choosing products designed for durability and reusability. Simple personal choices, buying second-hand, reducing food waste, or choosing repairable products, create a ripple effect of inspiring others. Think of Greta Thunberg, whose individual protests sparked a global climate movement.

   a. **Interactive Challenge**: What habit can you change today to align with circular principles? For instance, commit to carrying a reusable water bottle for a month and track its impact.

2. Professionals as Catalysts for Change

Professionals act as catalysts for circular practices because they influence, encourage, or speed up circularity. **Professionals across industries can embed circular principles in their work.** Architects can design buildings with modular components, technology leaders can innovate circular applications, and educators can inspire the next generation. For example, Levi's introduced a takeback programme to recycle old jeans, showcasing corporate leadership in circularity.

> **Example:** In Sweden, companies like IKEA are pivoting to circular models by renting furniture instead of selling it, illustrating how business innovation drives global impact.

3. Advocate for Policy and Community Engagement

Policy advocacy and community engagement serve as the driving forces in shaping a circular economy. Advocacy amplifies this effect. Encourage local governments to adopt circular policies or start grassroots initiatives. Cities such as Amsterdam pioneered circular economies through government-backed frameworks.

> b. **Practical Scenario**: Imagine joining a neighbourhood repair café to fix electronics and clothing and reduce waste while building community bonds.

4. Inspire Future Generations

Encouraging circular practices in future generations is crucial and can be achieved effectively if the current generation dedicates significant efforts to this goal. For the upcoming generations, these practices will become a practical approach, as they will have observed them from their predecessors. Consequently, they could easily relate to and implement these practices in their own lives.

Pass on the values of sustainability and stewardship by involving children and peers in circular practices. Schools in Japan teach recycling through creative art projects, ensuring circularity becomes second nature.

Sketch:

- A classroom where children are building products from recycled materials.
- A professional holding a briefcase marked "Circular Advocate."
- A family donating clothes with a sign reading, "Give, Don't Discard."

The call to action is simple but profound: **Be the spark that ignites the circular revolution.** Whether in your home, workplace, or community, your efforts can inspire others, creating a legacy of sustainability and shared prosperity. Together, we can turn aspiration into reality.

Recap and Summary:

1. The Path to a Fully Circular Economy:

Picture a future where products are crafted to last, materials are continuously recycled, and nothing goes to waste. Urban areas flourish on sustainable power sources, while industries embrace circular production methods. This vision is achieved through the combined efforts of people, corporations, and governing bodies.

2. Long-Term Benefits of Circularity:

The adoption of circular practices contributes to economic resilience by lessening reliance on resources, supports environmental restoration by revitalising ecosystems, and improves quality of life through fair and sustainable living conditions. Examples such as the circular policies implemented in Amsterdam demonstrate tangible positive outcomes.

3. Call to Action:

Each person has the power to support the circular economy through sustainable choices, workplace influence, and pushing for broader changes. From personal routines to professional advancements, these seemingly minor efforts collectively contribute to shaping a more sustainable, circular tomorrow.

Together, these elements inspire hope and actionable steps for realising a sustainable future.

CONCLUSION: THE WAY FORWARD FOR SUSTAINABLE PROGRESS

"Never doubt that a small group of thoughtful, committed citizens can change the world; indeed, it's the only thing that ever has."

— Margaret Mead

As we reach the final chapter of *Redesigning Prosperity*, it is time to reflect, recharge, and move forward with purpose. This conclusion weaves together the insights shared throughout the book, offering a vision of hope and actionable guidance for a sustainable future. By recapping key lessons, outlining practical steps, and sharing an empowering message, this chapter serves as both a roadmap and a rallying call. The journey to a circular, prosperous world begins with each of us, and together, we can shape a legacy of balance, innovation, and renewal. Let's take the first step, hand in hand.

Summary of key takeaways

As we revisit the journey of **Redesigning Prosperity**, we must synthesise the powerful ideas and actionable strategies explored throughout the book. After embracing these practices, the circular economy becomes the global standard, increasing employment and economic growth while reducing the use of scarce raw materials and mitigating the severe impact of emissions and climate change. This chapter weaves together the threads of our discussions, leaving readers equipped with a roadmap to adopt circularity in their lives and professions and redesign prosperity not only for the present but also for future generations.

1. Circular Economy's Core Concepts

The circular economy fundamentally challenges the traditional "take-make-waste" paradigm by promoting regenerative systems. Rather than viewing waste as an end result, circular concepts consider waste a valuable resource. This paradigm shift, akin to recalibrating a compass, reorients the definition of economic success to align it with environmental conservation. In doing so, it creates a new framework in which prosperity and sustainability are intrinsically linked.

- **Example:** IKEA's commitment to reduce operational waste by 90% shows the tangible impact of integrating circular principles into business practices.

Central Concept: Circularity extends beyond a mere idea; **it represents a comprehensive approach that separates economic advancement from environmental degradation, and presents a viable framework for sustainable development.**

2. Community and Individual Empowerment

Achieving sustainability requires united effort, with each person contributing significantly. The cumulative effect of minor actions, such as opting for products with eco-friendly labels, giving away unused possessions, or mending items instead of throwing them away, should not be underestimated. The family donating clothes, or a classroom teaching circular concepts to children, illustrates that the circular economy is not just about systems—it is about values. **In reality, these individual and community-based initiatives collectively generate substantial influence on attaining the intended outcome.**

Example: Repair cafes worldwide demonstrate the power of community-driven sustainability, where neighbours come together to fix household items, reduce waste, and foster collaboration.

Scenario: Picture a family hosting a garage sale and turning clutter into community wealth. These minor efforts embody the spirit of circularity.

Central Observation: By enabling and encouraging communities and individuals, the concept of circularity evolves from a broad systemic approach into a set of personal beliefs and practices, rendering sustainability more concrete and accessible.

3. Role of Measurement and Feedback

Metrics are the backbone of accountability in circular practices. Measurement and feedback provide us with information about things that are going in the right or wrong direction. These efforts are doing the right things or going in vain. From waste reduction rates to carbon footprint tracking, data-driven insights help stakeholders measure progress and refine strategies.

Example: Adidas' use of lifecycle analysis in sneaker production reduced emissions by 30%, demonstrating how data can drive innovation.

> **Scientific Evidence:** The Ellen MacArthur Foundation highlights that circular models can reduce global emissions by up to 39%.

Key Insight: Continuous learning through feedback loops ensures that circular systems evolve and thrive by adapting to new challenges and opportunities.

4. Overcoming Challenges with Solutions

The path to circularity is not without hurdles including cultural, economic, and regulatory barriers. However, creative solutions such as consumer education, public-private partnerships, and innovation incentives pave the way forward. All of these not only provide solutions for sustainability but also create a type of behaviour that becomes an inspiration for upcoming generations.

For example, Cities such as Amsterdam have implemented zero waste zones, supported by strong collaboration between businesses, governments, and communities.

Key Insight: Collaboration and innovation transform challenges into opportunities, demonstrating that barriers can be dismantled through strategic actions.

5. A Vision for the Future

Picture a world that embraces circular ideas: cities run on clean energy, factories produce no waste, and people thrive in harmony with nature. This is not just a dream—it is a real possibility based on what we are doing right now.

Central Idea: Going circular is the way to a better future bringing together a strong economy, a healthier planet, and happier people.

Sketch:

A dynamic collage depicting:

- A gearwheel symbolising the circular economy.
- Icons of solar panels, green factories, and thriving communities.
- A handshake representing partnerships.

The path ahead is obvious: circular thinking is not just an idea; it is a shift in how we do things. When we use these ideas to check how we affect things and team up, we can build a world were doing well goes hand in hand with helping the Earth. In the future, we want to hinge on what we decide to do right now.

Actionable Steps for Readers – A Guide to Getting Started with Circular Practices

Starting on the road to a circular economy might feel like you are looking at a blank map. But every big adventure begins with one small step, and this guide is here to light the way. Whether you are a person looking to make a real difference or a company wanting to change what success means, these practical steps give you a clear plan for a sustainable future.

1. Begin with Small Changes

Start by making simple everyday choices that align with circular principles. Opt for second-hand items, repair instead of replacing, or donate things that you no longer use.

- **Example:** Research shows that keeping clothes in use for just nine extra months reduces the environmental impact by up to 30%.
- **Idea:** Why do not host a clothing swap with friends? It is not only fun and eco-friendly but also builds a sense of community.

Takeaway: Small, consistent actions create a ripple effect that leads to significant change.

2. Share Knowledge and Inspire Others

It is true that awareness sparks actions. With the help of sharing knowledge, it is possible to inspire other for circular practices. Therefore, spread the word about circular practices within your circles—family, friends, colleagues, or online communities.

- **Example**: Repair cafes in Europe bring neighbours together to fix items and reduce waste while fostering collaboration and friendships.
- **Idea**: Organise a DIY workshop or share your own upcycling projects on social media.

Takeaway: Every conversation or shared tip can inspire someone else to take action. **By educating others, one can act as a catalyst for change.**

3. For Businesses: Start with an Audit

Businesses can make substantial contributions by assessing waste generation and resource usage to identify areas of improvement. Investigate methods to revise product designs, emphasising longevity, modular construction, and recyclability.

- **Case Study**: Philips adopted a circular approach by leasing lighting systems instead of selling bulbs, ensuring that the components were reused or upgraded.
- **Visual Idea**: Imagine a checklist that helps businesses explore areas such as waste reduction, product takeback programmes, and recycling partnerships.

Takeaway: Combining innovation with sustainability benefits the environment and generates financial gains.

4. Embrace Technology as a Tool for Change

Digital solutions are used to monitor and measure the progress. Apps, calculators, and tracking systems can make sustainability efforts more concrete and effective. Digital tools, such as lifecycle assessment (LCA) apps, carbon footprint calculators, and material tracking software, are used to monitor progress.

- **Example:** The app "Too Good To Go" connects users with surplus food from restaurants, reducing waste and saving money.

Takeaway: Technology simplifies the process of adopting circular practices, making it easier to see results and fill gaps between intentions and outcomes.

5. Join Forces and Collaborate

Changes do not occur during isolation. Partners with local groups, businesses, and policymakers to increase the impact. Join local sustainability initiatives, cooperate with like-minded organisations, and advocate supportive policies.

- **For example**, Amsterdam's success with its circular strategy highlights the power of collaboration between governments, businesses, and communities.

Takeaway: Together, we can achieve more than we can alone. **Collaboration is an engine of large-scale impacts that promotes innovation and shared resources.**

Moving Forward

The path to a circular economy does not require perfection, but just progress. Each choice, whether small or large, adds to the larger picture of a sustainable prosperous world. So why wait? Start today and be part of a movement that guarantees the well-being of both people and the planet.

Final Words on Redesigning Prosperity: A Vision of Hope and Action

As we come to the end of this journey, let us take a moment to imagine the future we can build together: a future where waste is transformed into an opportunity, where resources are restored instead of being exhausted, and where economic progress is no longer at odds with environmental health. **This concept of "Redesigning Prosperity" is not just about systems or policies; it is also about people, communities, and the choices we make every day.**

1. The Strength of Collective Action

The potential for achievement becomes apparent when individuals unite with common goals. Significant transformations are driven by the strength of cooperative efforts ranging from community-based projects to worldwide campaigns.

- **For example**, Copenhagen's goal of becoming the world's first carbon-neutral capital by 2025 is achieved through pioneering policies and active community participation.
- **Practical Scenario**: Think about a neighbourhood where families compost their kitchen waste to nurture urban gardens, creating greener, healthier spaces while reducing their environmental footprint.

2. A Circular Economy: Good for Everyone

Circularity is not just about saving the planet, it is about securing a better quality of life for everyone. **A circular world** creates economic opportunities, fosters innovation, and strengthens communities.

- **Scientific Insight**: According to the Ellen MacArthur Foundation, adopting circular principles could unlock $4.5 trillion in global economic benefits by 2030.
- **Metaphor**: Imagine a lifeline thrown to the planet and its people, a way to pull us out of the unsustainable cycle of take, make, and waste.

3. Turning Vision into Action

Bold, courageous steps are needed to bring this vision to life, but they begin with small, intentional actions. **It is possible that bold decisions may be required on a global scale, but progress starts with daily actions.**

- **Case Study**: Rwanda has become a global leader in sustainability, banning plastic bags and prioritising green development.
- **Interactive Idea**: Dear readers, you must document a specific eco-friendly action you can consistently perform, such as minimising the use of disposable plastics or patronising environmentally responsible companies, to convert your environmental aspirations into tangible results. Please judge your emotional response after completing your chosen commitment.

Visual Representation

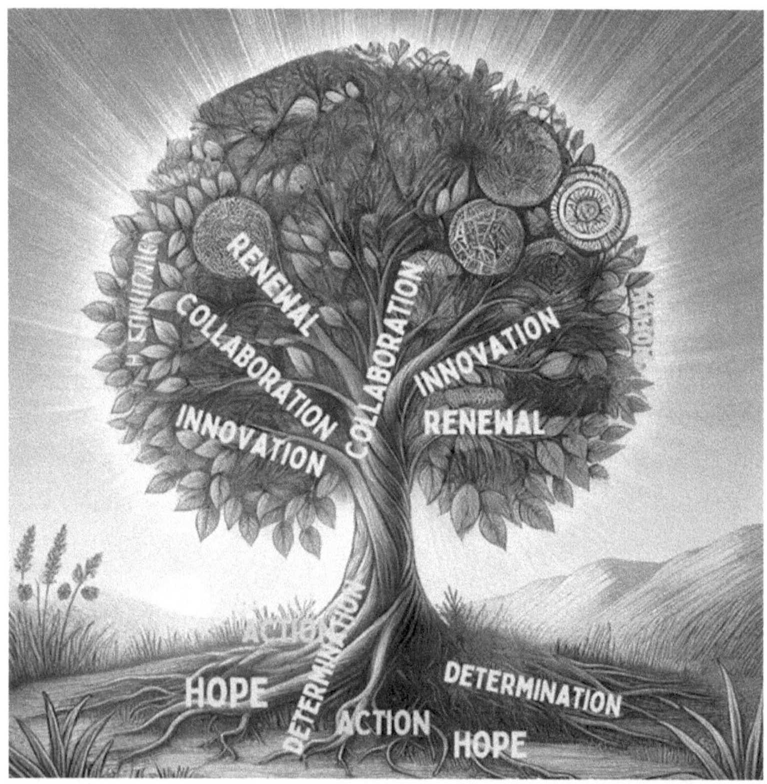

Imagine a tree growing from the Earth, its sturdy branches labelled with values like innovation, collaboration, and renewal, while its roots are anchored in hope, action, and determination.

Closing Words

This book is more than a guide—it is a call to action. **It is a reminder that we hold the power to create a world where economic prosperity and environmental sustainability coexist. The path forward is not without challenges, but together, through mindful choices and collective effort, we** can redesign prosperity for the generations to come. Let's start today.

For Redesigning Prosperity, it is important to **"Be a Performer, not a Spectator"**.

Recap and Summary:

As we bring *Redesigning Prosperity* to its conclusion, the vision for a circular future is clear. This chapter highlighted the transformative potential of embracing circular economy principles, not just as a framework but as a way of life. From revisiting the book's key takeaways to offering actionable steps, it served as a guide for individuals and businesses to align their choices with sustainable progress.

We explored how small, meaningful actions—like adopting zero waste practices or forming collaborations—can ripple out into significant societal change. The checklist provided practical tools to get started, while **the empowering final message urged readers to think boldly, act responsibly, and champion the circular movement in every facet of their lives.**

This chapter serves as both a conclusion and a call to action, leaving readers inspired to contribute to a prosperous, sustainable world. **Together, we can transform today's challenges into tomorrow's opportunities.**

REFERENCES

Introduction

1. Ellen MacArthur Foundation. (2019). **"Circular Economy: A Vision for a Sustainable Future."** Retrieved from https://www.ellenmacarthurfoundation.org

2. United Nations Department of Economic and Social Affairs (UNDESA). (2018). **"World Population Prospects: The 2018 Revision."** Retrieved from https://www.un.org/development/desa/publications

3. World Economic Forum. (2021). **"The Circularity Gap Report."** Retrieved from https://www.circularity-gap.world

4. WHO. (2021). **"Air Pollution: Key Facts and Statistics."** Retrieved from https://www.who.int/news-room/fact-sheets/detail/air-pollution

5. Jambeck, J. R., et al. (2015). **"Plastic Waste Inputs from Land into the Ocean."** *Science*, 347(6223), 768-771. DOI: 10.1126/science.1260352

6. Philips. (2020). **"Sustainability Report 2020."** Retrieved from https://www.philips.com

7. Stahel, W. R. (2016). **"The Circular Economy: A User's Guide."** *Nature*, 531(7595), 435-438. DOI: 10.1038/531435a

8. European Commission. (2020). **"A New Circular Economy Action Plan for a Cleaner and More**

Competitive Europe." Retrieved from https://ec.europa.eu/environment/circular-economy/

9. Geissdoerfer, M., Savaget, P., Bocken, N. M. P., & Hultink, E. J. (2017). **"The Circular Economy – A New Sustainability Paradigm?"** *Journal of Cleaner Production,* 143, 757–768. DOI: 10.1016/j.jclepro.2016.12.048

10. PACE (Platform for Accelerating the Circular Economy). (2021). **"The Circular Economy Handbook."** Retrieved from https://pacecircular.org

11. McDonough, W., & Braungart, M. (2002). **"Cradle to Cradle: Remaking the Way We Make Things."** North Point Press.

12. Jack Canfield **"Success Principles"**

13. United Nations Environment Programme (UNEP). (2019). **"Global Resources Outlook 2019: Natural Resources for the Future We Want."** Retrieved from https://www.unep.org/resources/global-resources-outlook

14. The Brundtland Report, officially titled "Our Common Future," was published in 1987 by the World Commission on Environment and Development (WCED)

Chapter 1

1. **On Linear Economy and Resource Depletion**

    a. Ellen MacArthur Foundation. (2013). *Towards the Circular Economy Vol. 1: Economic and Business Rationale for an Accelerated Transition.* Available at: https://ellenmacarthurfoundation.org

    b. Meadows, D. H., Meadows, D. L., Randers, J., & Behrens III, W. W. (1972). *The Limits to Growth.* Potomac Associates.

2. **Environmental Impacts of Linear Models**

   a. United Nations Environment Programme (UNEP). (2021). *Global Resources Outlook 2019: Natural Resources for the Future We Want.* Available at: https://www.resourcepanel.org/reports

   b. Geyer, R., Jambeck, J. R., & Law, K. L. (2017). *Production, Use, and Fate of All Plastics Ever Made.* Science Advances, 3(7), e1700782. DOI: 10.1126/sciadv.1700782

3. **Economic Instability from Finite Resources**

   a. International Monetary Fund (IMF). (2021). *Commodity Market Outlook.* Available at: https://www.imf.org

   b. World Economic Forum. (2020). *The Future of Nature and Business.* Available at: https://www.weforum.org/reports

4. **Case Examples of Circular Practices**

   a. Stahel, W. R. (2016). *The Circular Economy: A User's Guide.* Routledge.

   b. Kirchherr, J., Reike, D., & Hekkert, M. (2017). *Conceptualizing the Circular Economy: An Analysis of 114 Definitions.* Resources, Conservation and Recycling, 127, 221-232. DOI: 10.1016/j.resconrec.2017.09.005

5. **Plastic Pollution and Examples**

   a. Lebreton, L., & Andrady, A. (2019). *Future Scenarios of Global Plastic Waste Generation and*

Disposal. Palgrave Communications, 5(6). DOI: 10.1057/s41599-018-0212-7

b. Great Pacific Garbage Patch. (2021). The Ocean Cleanup Project. Available at: https://theoceancleanup.com

6. **Circular Economy Opportunities and Impacts**

a. World Economic Forum and Ellen MacArthur Foundation. (2014). *Towards the Circular Economy: Accelerating the Scale Up Across Global Supply Chains.* Available at: https://ellenmacarthurfoundation.org

b. The World Bank. (2018). *What a Waste 2.0: A Global Snapshot of Solid Waste Management to 2050.* Available at: https://datatopics.worldbank.org

7. **Social Impacts of Linear Models**

a. World Health Organisation (WHO). (2021). *Air Pollution and Health.* Available at: https://www.who.int/airpollution

b. UN Department of Economic and Social Affairs. (2020). *World Social Report 2020: Inequality in a Rapidly Changing World.* Available at: https://www.un.org/development

8. **Economic Benefits of Circular Economy**

a. Accenture. (2015). *Waste to Wealth: Creating Advantage in a Circular Economy.* Palgrave Macmillan.

b. McKinsey & Company. (2016). *The Circular Economy: Moving From Theory to Practice*. Available at: https://www.mckinsey.com

9. **Interactive Prompts and Sustainability Practices**

a. Thiele, L. P. (2016). *Sustainability*. Polity Press.

b. UNEP. (2021). *Turning the Tide on Single-Use Plastics*. Available at: https://www.unep.org

10. **Regenerative Agriculture**

a. Lal, R. (2020). *Regenerative Agriculture for Food and Climate*. Journal of Soil and Water Conservation, 75(5), 123A–124A. DOI: 10.2489/jswc.2020.0620A

11. **Future Prospects for Circular Economy**

a. Raworth, K. (2017). *Doughnut Economics: Seven Ways to Think Like a 21st-Century Economist*. Chelsea Green Publishing.

b. Preston, F. (2012). *A Global Redesign? Shaping the Circular Economy*. Chatham House Briefing Paper. Available at: https://www.chathamhouse.org

12. "The 7 Habits of Highly Effective People" by Stephen R. Covey

Chapter 2

1. **Ellen MacArthur Foundation**. (2013). *Towards the Circular Economy: Economic and Business Rationale for an Accelerated Transition*. Retrieved from https://ellenmacarthurfoundation.org

2. **World Economic Forum.** (2020). *The Future of the Circular Economy: Trends and Opportunities.* Retrieved from https://www.weforum.org

3. **Adidas.** (2019). *Futurecraft Loop: Creating the First Recyclable Performance Running Shoe.* Retrieved from https://www.adidas-group.com

4. **Tesla, Inc.** (2022). *Closed-Loop Battery Recycling in Gigafactory Operations.* Retrieved from https://www.tesla.com

5. **Caterpillar.** (2021). *Remanufacturing Solutions: Driving Sustainability Through Innovation.* Retrieved from https://www.caterpillar.com

6. Ghisellini, P., Cialani, C., & Ulgiati, S. (2016). A review on circular economy: The expected transition to a balanced interplay of environmental and economic systems. *Journal of Cleaner Production, 114,* 11-32. https://doi.org/10.1016/j.jclepro.2015.09.007

7. **Ellen MacArthur Foundation.** (2021). *Circular Economy in Action: Case Studies of Innovation Across Industries.* Retrieved from https://ellenmacarthurfoundation.org

8. **Patagonia.** (2019). *Worn Wear: Building Loyalty Through Repair and Sustainability.* Retrieved from https://www.patagonia.com

9. **Denmark's Kalundborg Eco-Industrial Park.** (2020). *Collaborative Solutions for a Circular Future.* Retrieved from https://stateofgreen.com

10. **International Labour Organisation.** (2021). *Promoting Social Inclusion Through Circular Economy Practices.* Retrieved from https://www.ilo.org

11. **World Bank**. (2022). *Waste Management in India: Scaling Circular Practices in Urban Areas.* Retrieved from https://www.worldbank.org

12. Stahel, W. R. (2019). *The Circular Economy: A User's Guide.* Routledge.

13. **UNEP**. (2021). *Advancing Resource Efficiency in Global Industries: A Guide to Circular Economy Best Practices.* Retrieved from https://www.unep.org

14. **McKinsey & Company**. (2016). *The Circular Economy: Moving From Theory to Practice.* Retrieved from https://www.mckinsey.com

15. **Airbnb**. (2021). *Sharing Economy Models: A Sustainable Future Through Collaboration.* Retrieved from https://www.airbnb.com

16. **Uber**. (2020). *Reducing Emissions Through Shared Mobility: Environmental Impact Reports.* Retrieved from https://www.uber.com

17. **Circular Economy in India**. (2021). *Integrating the Informal Sector in Circular Waste Management.* Retrieved from https://www.ceinindia.org

18. **Philips Lighting**. (2019). *Lighting as a Service: A Model for a Sustainable Future.* Retrieved from https://www.signify.com

19. **National Geographic**. (2019). *Rivers Reborn: The Environmental Benefits of Circular Practices.* Retrieved from https://www.nationalgeographic.com

20. **OECD**. (2022). *Circular Economy Strategies for Resource Efficiency and Waste Reduction.* Retrieved from https://www.oecd.org

Chapter3

Books

1. Ellen MacArthur Foundation. (2015). *Towards the Circular Economy: Economic and Business Rationale for an Accelerated Transition.* Ellen MacArthur Foundation Publishing.
2. McDonough, W., & Braungart, M. (2002). *Cradle to Cradle: Remaking the Way We Make Things.* North Point Press.
3. Stahel, W. R. (2016). *The Circular Economy: A User's Guide.* Routledge.

Academic Articles

1. Ghisellini, P., Cialani, C., & Ulgiati, S. (2016). A review on circular economy: The expected transition to a balanced interplay of environmental and economic systems. *Journal of Cleaner Production, 114,* 11-32. https://doi.org/10.1016/j.jclepro.2015.09.007
2. Korhonen, J., Nuur, C., Feldmann, A., & Birkie, S. E. (2018). Circular economy as an essentially contested concept. *Journal of Cleaner Production, 175,* 544-552. https://doi.org/10.1016/j.jclepro.2017.12.111

Case Studies

1. **Singapore's NEWater:**

   a. Public Utilities Board (PUB). (2021). *NEWater: Singapore's Success Story in Water Reclamation.* Retrieved from https://www.pub.gov.sg

2. **Econyl – Nylon from Waste:**

   a. Aquafil Group. (2020). *Econyl: Nylon Regeneration System.* Retrieved from https://www.econyl.com

3. **Dell Technologies – E-Waste Management:**

   a. Dell Technologies Sustainability Reports (2021). Available at https://corporate.delltechnologies.com

Reports

1. World Economic Forum, Ellen MacArthur Foundation, & McKinsey & Company. (2016). *The New Plastics Economy: Rethinking the Future of Plastics.* Available at https://ellenmacarthurfoundation.org
2. UN Environment Programme (UNEP). (2021). *The Role of Circular Economy in Sustainable Development.* Available at https://www.unep.org

Web Resources

1. TerraCycle Official Website: https://www.terracycle.com
2. Gjenge Makers (Plastic Paving Bricks in Kenya): https://gjenge.com
3. AgriProtein Official Website (Turning Waste to Animal Feed): https://agriprotein.com

Statistics and Data Sources

1. OECD. (2019). *Global Material Resources Outlook to 2060: Economic Drivers and Environmental Consequences.* https://www.oecd.org

2. Statista. (2023). Recycling rates worldwide: https://www.statista.com

Other Resources

1. Videos:

    a. Ellen MacArthur Foundation (YouTube Channel): Insightful videos on circular economy case studies. https://www.youtube.com/user/made2bemadeagain

2. Documentaries:

    a. *Closing the Loop* (2018): A documentary on the circular economy directed by Graham Sheldon and Wayne Visser.

Chapter 4

Durability

1. **Patagonia Case Study**

    a. Patagonia. (n.d.). *Repair and Care Programme.* Retrieved from https://www.patagonia.com
    b. Schendler, A., & Toffel, M. W. (2021). *The Sustainable Business Handbook: A Guide to Becoming More Innovative, Resilient, and Successful.*

Modularity

2. **Fairphone Case Study**

    a. Fairphone. (n.d.). *Our Mission: A Fairer Future for Electronics.* Retrieved from https://www.fairphone.com

b. Jones, P., Hillier, D., & Comfort, D. (2020). *The sustainable development goals and the electronic industry.* Management Research Review, 43(4), 423-442.

Recyclability

1. **IKEA Case Study**

    a. IKEA. (2022). *Sustainability Report FY22.* Retrieved from https://www.ikea.com

    b. De Jong, S., & Tromp, N. (2020). *Design for recyclability: Circular innovation in furniture.* Design Studies, 68, 35-50.

2. **Loop Case Study**

    a. Loop. (2023). *Sustainable Packaging Solutions.* Retrieved from https://www.loopstore.com

    b. TerraCycle. (2021). *The Loop Partnership Model.* Retrieved from https://www.terracycle.com

Closed-Loop Systems

1. **Interface Case Study**

    a. Interface. (2022). *Climate Take Back Programme.* Retrieved from https://www.interface.com

    b. Anderson, R. (2009). *Confessions of a Radical Industrialist: Profits, People, Purpose - Doing Business by Respecting the Earth.*

Designing for Circularity

1. **Apple Case Study**

   a. Apple. (2022). *Environmental Progress Report.* Retrieved from https://www.apple.com

   b. Puckett, J., & Smith, T. (2021). *The challenges of designing sustainable electronics.* Journal of Industrial Ecology, 25(4), 717-730.

Material Innovation

1. **Carlsberg Case Study**

   a. Carlsberg. (2023). *Sustainability Report: Green Fibre Bottle Initiative.* Retrieved from https://www.carlsberggroup.com

   b. White, M. A. (2020). *Innovation for sustainability in packaging design.* Packaging Technology and Science, 33(3), 107-121.

Business Model Evolution

1. **Rolls-Royce Case Study**

   a. Rolls-Royce. (2023). *Sustainability and Innovation in Aviation.* Retrieved from https://www.rolls-royce.com

   b. Stahel, W. R. (2019). *The Circular Economy: A User's Guide.*

Collaboration as a Catalyst

1. **Ellen MacArthur Foundation**

   a. Ellen MacArthur Foundation. (2023). *The Circular Economy in Action: Case Studies.* Retrieved from https://www.ellenmacarthurfoundation.org

   b. Webster, K. (2017). *The Circular Economy: A Wealth of Flows.* 2nd Edition.

Chapter 5

1. Ellen MacArthur Foundation. (2021). *The circular economy in detail.* Retrieved from https://ellenmacarthurfoundation.org

2. Philips Lighting. (2016). *Lighting as a Service: Pioneering sustainable solutions for a circular future.* Retrieved from https://www.philips.com

3. Signify. (2018). *Circular economy in practice: Lighting as a Service at Schiphol Airport.* Retrieved from https://www.signify.com

4. **IKEA Official Report:** IKEA. (2020). *Sustainability and circular business strategy: Extending product lifecycles with our Buy-Back program.* Retrieved from https://www.ikea.com

5. **Third-Party Analysis:** Ellen MacArthur Foundation. (2019). *Circular design in practice: How IKEA's Buy-Back program transforms waste into value.* Retrieved from https://ellenmacarthurfoundation.org

6. Guttentag, D. (2015). Airbnb: Disruptive innovation and the rise of an informal tourism accommodation sector. *Current Issues in Tourism, 18*(12), 1192–1217. https://doi.org/10.1080/13683500.2014.958610

7. Ert, E., Fleischer, A., & Magen, N. (2016). Trust and reputation in the sharing economy: The role of personal photos in Airbnb. *Tourism Management, 55,* 62–73. https://doi.org/10.1016/j.tourman.2016.01.001

8. **Shaheen, S., Guzman, S., & Zhang, H. (2010).** Bikesharing in Europe, the Americas, and Asia: Past,

present, and future. *Transportation Research Record, 2143*(1), 159–167. https://doi.org/10.3141/2143-17

9. **Fishman, E. (2016).** Bikeshare: A review of recent literature. *Transport Reviews, 36*(1), 92–113. https://doi.org/10.1080/01441647.2015.1033036

10. European Environment Agency. (2021). *Circular economy strategies and greenhouse gas emissions.* Retrieved from https://www.eea.europa.eu

11. Interface. (2020). *Mission Zero progress report.* Retrieved from https://www.interface.com

12. Lund, R. (2018). *The remanufacturing industry: Hidden giant.* Boston University Press.

13. OECD. (2022). *Public-private partnerships for circular economy innovation.* Retrieved from https://www.oecd.org

14. Patagonia. (2023). *Worn wear initiative: Promoting sustainable fashion.* Retrieved from https://www.patagonia.com

15. Renault. (2021). *Sustainability report: Circular manufacturing and remanufacturing.* Retrieved from https://group.renault.com

16. Unilever. (2022). *Sustainable living brands: Love Beauty and Planet.* Retrieved from https://www.unilever.com

17. World Economic Forum. (2023). *The future of circular business models: Opportunities and challenges.* Retrieved from https://www.weforum.org

Chapter 6

1. European Union's Circular Economy Action Plan (CEAP):

European Commission. (2020). *Circular economy action plan: For a cleaner and more competitive Europe.* European Commission. Retrieved from https://environment.ec.europa. eu/strategy/circular-economy-action-plan_en

European Commission. (2020). *A new circular economy action plan for a cleaner and more competitive Europe* [PDF]. Retrieved from https://eur-lex.europa.eu/resource.html ?format=PDF&uri=cellar%3A9903b325-6388-11ea-b735-01aa75ed71a1.0017.02%2FDOC_1

2. Japan's Home Appliance Recycling Law:

Ministry of the Environment, Japan. (2021). *Home appliance recycling law and its implementation.* Retrieved from https:// www.env.go.jp/content/900452888.pdf

Panasonic Eco. (n.d.). *Home appliance recycling in Japan.* Panasonic Corporation. Retrieved from https://panasonic. net/eco/petec/recycle/

3. Singapore's Zero Waste Master Plan:

National Environment Agency, Singapore. (2019). *Zero waste masterplan: A sustainable Singapore.* Singapore Government. Retrieved from https://www.nea.gov.sg/our-services/waste-management/3r-programmes-and-resources/zero-waste-masterplan

4. India's Extended Producer Responsibility (EPR) Framework:

Ministry of Environment, Forest and Climate Change, India. (2022). *Extended producer responsibility (EPR) for plastic waste management.* Retrieved from https://moef.gov.in/wp-content/uploads/2022/02/EPR-Guidelines-Plastic.pdf

5. Finland's Construction Waste Reduction Initiatives:

European Environment Agency. (2021). *Finland's circular economy roadmap and construction waste reduction initiatives.* Retrieved from https://www.eea.europa.eu/publications/circular-economy-in-europe

6. The Closed-Loop Fund in the USA:

Closed-Loop Partners. (2022). *The closed-loop infrastructure fund: A scalable solution for recycling investment in the USA.* Retrieved from https://www.closedlooppartners.com/funds/infrastructure/

- **Sweden:**

  Sitra. (2021). *The circular economy in Sweden: Promoting repair and reuse.* Retrieved from https://www.sitra.fi/en/

- **Netherlands:**

  City of Amsterdam. (2021). *Circular Amsterdam: A roadmap towards a 100% circular city by 2050.* Retrieved from https://www.amsterdam.nl/en/policy/sustainability/

- **India:**

  Ministry of Environment, Forest and Climate Change, Government of India. (2016). *E-Waste Management Rules, 2016*. Retrieved from http://moef.gov.in

- **China:**

  Government of the People's Republic of China. (2018). *Circular Economy Promotion Law*. Retrieved from http://www.gov.cn

- **France:**

  Ministry for the Ecological Transition, France. (2020). *Anti-Waste Law for a Circular Economy*. Retrieved from https://www.ecologie.gouv.fr

- **South Korea:**

  Ministry of Environment, South Korea. (2020). *Resource Circulation Policy*. Retrieved from https://www.me.go.kr

- **Germany:**

  Federal Ministry for the Environment, Nature Conservation and Nuclear Safety, Germany. (2019). *Closed Substance Cycle and Waste Management Act*. Retrieved from https://www.bmu.de

- **Kenya:**

  National Environment Management Authority. (2017). *Plastic Bag Ban*. Retrieved from https://www.nema.go.ke

Chapter 7

1. Consumer Demand for Sustainable Products

- Nielsen. (2018). *The evolution of the sustainability mindset.* Retrieved from https://www.nielsen.com/us/en/insights/report/2018/the-evolution-of-the-sustainability-mindset

2. Patagonia's "Worn Wear" Programme

- Patagonia. (n.d.). *Worn wear: Better than new.* Retrieved from https://wornwear.patagonia.com

3. Circular Lifestyles and Fashion Rental Platforms

- ThredUp. (2022). *2022 resale report: The latest trends in second-hand fashion.* Retrieved from https://www.thredup.com/resale
- Rent the Runway. (n.d.). *How it works.* Retrieved from https://www.renttherunway.com

4. Community Engagement in Zero Waste Initiatives

- Zero Waste International Alliance. (2021). *What is zero waste?* Retrieved from https://zwia.org/zero-waste-definition

5. Education and Cultural Shifts Toward Circularity

- Finnish National Agency for Education. (2021). *Sustainability in education: Finland's approach to circular economy learning.* Retrieved from https://www.oph.fi/en

6. Public-Private Partnerships in Circular Awareness Campaigns

- Coca-Cola. (2021). *World without waste: Our commitment to sustainability.* Retrieved from https://www.coca-colacompany.com/sustainable-business/world-without-waste

7. Digital Awareness Campaigns on Sustainability

- Plastic Free July Foundation. (n.d.). *Plastic Free July: Be part of the solution.* Retrieved from https://www.plasticfreejuly.org
- The True Cost. (2015). *The true cost* [Documentary]. Life is My Movie Entertainment.

8. Hands-on Circular Workshops and Experiential Learning

- Kolb, D. A. (1984). *Experiential learning: Experience as the source of learning and development.* Prentice Hall.

9. Responsible Consumption and Extended Product Lifespan

- WRAP. (2017). *Extending product lifetimes: Environmental and economic benefits.* Retrieved from https://www.wrap.org.uk/sustainable-product-design

10. Reuse and Repair Economy

- European Environment Agency. (2020). *A framework for circular economy indicators.* Retrieved from https://www.eea.europa.eu/publications/circular-economy-indicators

11. Recycling and Waste Reduction Best Practices

- Ellen MacArthur Foundation. (2019). *Completing the picture: How the circular economy tackles climate change.* Retrieved from https://ellenmacarthurfoundation.org/resources

- City of San Francisco. (2020). *Zero waste by 2030: San Francisco's waste management plan.* Retrieved from https://sfenvironment.org/zero-waste

12. The sharing economy and Second-hand Shopping

- Botsman, R., & Rogers, R. (2010). *What is mine is yours: The rise of collaborative consumption.* Harper Business.

- Patagonia. (n.d.). *Worn wear: Keeping gear in play.* Retrieved from https://wornwear.patagonia.com

- BorrowMyStuff. (n.d.). *How borrowing saves money and the planet.* Retrieved from https://www.borrowmystuff.com

Chapter 8

1. **Ellen MacArthur Foundation.** (2021). *Completing the picture: How the circular economy tackles climate change.* Retrieved from https://ellenmacarthurfoundation.org/completing-the-picture

2. **Geyer, R., Jambeck, J. R., & Law, K. L.** (2017). Production, use, and fate of all plastics ever made. *Science Advances, 3*(7), e1700782. https://doi.org/10.1126/sciadv.1700782

3. **Greenhouse Gas Protocol.** (2004). *A corporate accounting and reporting standard.* World Resources Institute & World Business Council for Sustainable

Development. Retrieved from https://ghgprotocol.org/corporate-standard

4. **IKEA.** (2021). *Sustainability Report FY21: Circular and climate positive.* Retrieved from https://www.ikea.com/global/en/sustainability

5. **MIT Sloan School of Management.** (2020). *The role of feedback loops in adaptive business models.* Retrieved from https://mitsloan.mit.edu

6. **Microsoft.** (2022). *2022 Environmental Sustainability Report: Carbon accounting and climate goals.* Retrieved from https://www.microsoft.com/sustainability

7. **Renault Group.** (2021). *Circular economy and remanufacturing: Renault's sustainable strategy.* Retrieved from https://www.renaultgroup.com/en/sustainability

8. **The Circularity Gap Report.** (2023). *Circular economy progress and global assessment.* Circle Economy Foundation. Retrieved from https://www.circularity-gap.world/2023

9. **Unilever.** (2021). *Life Cycle Assessment in Sustainable Product Development.* Retrieved from https://www.unilever.com/sustainable-living

10. **United Nations Environment Programme (UNEP).** (2021). *Global Waste Management Outlook: Circular economy and waste reduction.* Retrieved from https://www.unep.org/resources

11. **Walmart.** (2022). *Blockchain technology in supply chain transparency.* Retrieved from https://corporate.walmart.com

Chapter 9

Academic & Industry Reports

1. Ellen MacArthur Foundation. (2013). *Towards the Circular Economy: Economic and Business Rationale for an Accelerated Transition.* Retrieved from https://ellenmacarthurfoundation.org

2. McKinsey & Company. (2016). *The Circular Economy: Moving from Theory to Practice.* Retrieved from https://www.mckinsey.com

3. Organisation for Economic Co-operation and Development (OECD). (2021). *Green Growth and Circular Economy Policies.* Retrieved from https://www.oecd.org/environment/

4. World Economic Forum (WEF). (2021). *Harnessing the Fourth Industrial Revolution for the Circular Economy.* Retrieved from https://www.weforum.org

5. European Commission. (2020). *A New Circular Economy Action Plan: For a Cleaner and More Competitive Europe.* Retrieved from https://ec.europa.eu/environment/circular-economy/

Case Studies & Corporate Initiatives

1. **Unilever's Packaging Transition**

   a. Unilever. (2020). *Plastic Packaging and Sustainability Initiatives.* Retrieved from https://www.unilever.com

2. **India's E-Waste Management Rules (2016)**

   a. Ministry of Environment, Forest and Climate Change (MoEFCC), Government of India. (2016).

E-Waste (Management) Rules, 2016. Retrieved from http://moef.gov.in

3. **Sweden's Repair Tax Rebates**

    a. Swedish Tax Agency. (2017). *Tax Deductions for Repairs to Reduce Waste.* Retrieved from https://www.skatteverket.se

4. **Ellen MacArthur Foundation – CE100 Initiative**

    a. Ellen MacArthur Foundation. (2018). *CE100 Programme: Driving Collaborative Innovation for a Circular Economy.* Retrieved from https://ellenmacarthurfoundation.org/ce100

5. **Coca-Cola & Veolia Bottle-to-Bottle Recycling**

    a. Veolia. (2021). *Building a Circular Plastic Economy with Coca-Cola.* Retrieved from https://www.veolia.com

Technological Innovations in Circular Economy

1. **LanzaTech's Carbon Recycling Technology**

- LanzaTech. (2021). *Turning Carbon Emissions into Sustainable Fuels & Chemicals.* Retrieved from https://www.lanzatech.com

2. **IBM's Blockchain for Food Waste Reduction**

- IBM. (2019). *Food Trust Blockchain Initiative: Reducing Waste in Supply Chains.* Retrieved from https://www.ibm.com/blockchain/solutions/food-trust

3. **AMP Robotics' AI Sorting Technology**

- AMP Robotics. (2020). *Revolutionising Waste Sorting with AI & Machine Learning.* Retrieved from https://www.amprobotics.com

4. **McKinsey's Digital Efficiency Report**

- McKinsey & Company. (2020). *How Digital Innovation Can Reduce Material Waste by 30%.* Retrieved from https://www.mckinsey.com

Chapter 10

1. **Ellen MacArthur Foundation.** (2020). *The Circular Economy: A Transformative Approach to Sustainability.* Retrieved from https://ellenmacarthurfoundation.org
2. **Accenture Strategy.** (2021). *Waste to Wealth: Creating Advantage in a Circular Economy.* Accenture. Retrieved from https://www.accenture.com
3. **Swedish Waste Management Association.** (2022). *Waste Management in Sweden: Towards Zero Landfill.* Retrieved from https://www.avfallsverige.se
4. **Interface Carpets.** (2023). *Recycling for a Sustainable Future: The Story of Interface Carpets.* Retrieved from https://www.interface.com
5. **City of Amsterdam.** (2021). *Amsterdam Circular: A Vision and Strategy for 2050.* Retrieved from https://www.amsterdam.nl
6. **Circularise.** (2023). *How Blockchain and Digital Platforms Enable Circular Economy.* Retrieved from https://www.circularise.com

7. **United Nations Environment Programme (UNEP).** (2022). *Shaping a Sustainable Future: The Role of Cultural Shifts in Circular Economy.* Retrieved from https://www.unep.org

8. **The Ellen MacArthur Foundation.** (2019). *Regenerative Agriculture: Principles for a Circular Food System.* Retrieved from https://ellenmacarthurfoundation.org

9. **The Netherlands Ministry of Infrastructure and Water Management.** (2021). *Circular Economy in the Dutch Construction Sector: Policies and Progress.* Retrieved from https://www.government.nl

10. **World Economic Forum.** (2020). *Circular Business Models: Unlocking a $4.5 Trillion Opportunity.* Retrieved from https://www.weforum.org

11. **IKEA Sustainability Report.** (2023). *From Linear to Circular: IKEA's Approach to Circular Business Models.* Retrieved from https://www.ikea.com

12. **Greta Thunberg & Fridays for Future.** (2019). *How Individual Actions Can Drive Systemic Change.* Retrieved from https://fridaysforfuture.org

13. **Japan Ministry of the Environment.** (2022). *Mottainai: The Japanese Approach to Waste Reduction and Resource Efficiency.* Retrieved from https://www.env.go.jp

14. **European Commission.** (2021). *The Role of Policy in Enabling a Circular Economy.* Retrieved from https://ec.europa.eu

15. **Levi Strauss & Co.** (2022). *Circular Fashion: How Levi's Takeback Programme Supports Sustainability.* Retrieved from https://www.levi.com

Conclusion

Academic and Industry Reports:

1. Ellen MacArthur Foundation. (2019). Completing the picture: How the circular economy tackles climate change. Retrieved from https://ellenmacarthurfoundation.org/completing-the-picture

2. Ellen MacArthur Foundation. (2021). Universal circular economy policy goals. Retrieved from https://ellenmacarthurfoundation.org/universal-circular-economy-policy-goals

3. World Economic Forum. (2021). The circular economy handbook: Realising the circular advantage. Retrieved from https://www.weforum.org/reports/the-circular-economy-handbook

4. United Nations Environment Programme (UNEP). (2020). The circularity gap report. Retrieved from https://www.circularity-gap.world/

5. Organisation for Economic Co-operation and Development (OECD). (2020). The circular economy in cities and regions. Retrieved from https://www.oecd.org/regional/circular-economy-cities.htm

Case Studies and Business Reports:

1. IKEA. (2023). Circular and climate positive strategy. Retrieved from https://www.ikea.com/global/en/newsroom/circular-sustainability-strategy

2. Adidas. (2022). Sustainability progress report: Moving towards a circular future. Retrieved from https://www.adidas-group.com/en/sustainability/reporting/

3. Philips. (2021). Circular economy at Philips: From selling products to providing services. Retrieved from https://www.philips.com/a-w/about/sustainability/circular-economy.html

4. Too Good To Go. (2023). Fighting food waste with technology. Retrieved from https://toogoodtogo.com/en-us

5. City of Amsterdam. (2020). Amsterdam circular 2020-2025 strategy. Retrieved from https://www.amsterdam.nl/en/policy/sustainability/circular-economy/

Scientific Research and Articles:

1. WRAP. (2017). Extending the life of clothes: Environmental benefits. Retrieved from https://www.wrap.org.uk/sustainable-textiles/clothing-life-extension

2. Stahel, W. R. (2016). The circular economy: A user's guide. Nature, 531(7595), 435-438. https://doi.org/10.1038/531435a

3. Ghisellini, P., Cialani, C., & Ulgiati, S. (2016). A review on circular economy: The expected transition to a balanced interplay of environmental and economic systems. Journal of Cleaner Production, 114, 11-32. https://doi.org/10.1016/j.jclepro.2015.09.007

4. European Commission. (2020). A new circular economy action plan for a cleaner and more competitive Europe. Retrieved from https://ec.europa.eu/environment/circular-economy/

5. City of Copenhagen. (2025). Copenhagen climate plan 2025: Becoming the world's first carbon-neutral capital.

Retrieved from https://urbandevelopmentcph.kk.dk/artikel/climate-plan-2025

Government and Nonprofit Reports:

1. Rwanda Environment Management Authority. (2021). Rwanda's plastic ban and green growth strategy. Retrieved from https://rema.gov.rw
2. World Bank. (2021). Circular economy in developing countries: Unlocking growth and sustainability. Retrieved from https://www.worldbank.org/en/topic/circulareconomy

ABOUT THE AUTHOR

Dr. Meenakshi Srivastava is an economist with a heart for sustainability and a mind for innovative solutions. With a Ph.D. in Economics focusing on sustainable development, she brings together years of academic research and a deep passion for creating positive change. Currently working at the Indian Institute of Management Bangalore (IIMB) as an Academic Associate, Dr. Meenakshi spends her time teaching, mentoring, and exploring new ways to make the circular economy a reality. Through this book, she hopes to inspire readers—from policymakers to everyday people—to take small but impactful steps toward a future that benefits both people and the planet.

Write to Dr. Meenakshi
meenakshi.srivastava1506@gmail.com